ORDINARY PEOPLE,

EXTRAORDINARY

WEALTH

P9-DGB-275

ORDINARY PEOPLE, EXTRAORDINARY WEALTH

The 8 Secrets of How 5,000
Ordinary Americans Became
Successful Investors
– And How You Can Too

Ric Edelman, CFS, RFC, CMFC

HarperBusiness
An Imprint of HarperCollins*Publishers*

Presentation of performance data does not imply that similar results will be achieved in the future. Rather, past performance is no indication of future results and any assertion to the contrary is a federal offense. Any such data is provided merely for illustrative and discussion purposes; rather than focusing on the time periods used or the results derived, the reader should focus instead on the underlying principles.

None of the material presented here is intended to serve as the basis for any financial decision, nor does any of the information contained within constitute an offer to buy or sell any security. Such an offer is made only by prospectus, which you should read carefully before investing or sending money.

The material presented in this book is accurate to the best of my knowledge. However, performance data changes over time, and laws frequently change as well, and my advice could change accordingly. Therefore, the reader is encouraged to verify the status of such information before acting.

ORDINARY PEOPLE, EXTRAORDINARY WEALTH. Copyright © 2000, 2001 by Ric Edelman. All rights reserved. Printed in the United States of America. No part of this book may be used or reproduced in any manner whatsoever without written permission except in the case of brief quotations embodied in critical articles and reviews. For information address HarperCollins Publishers Inc., 10 East 53rd Street, New York, NY 10022.

HarperCollins books may be purchased for educational, business, or sales promotional use. For information please write: Special Markets Department, HarperCollins Publishers Inc., 10 East 53rd Street, New York, NY 10022.

Designed by Ric Edelman and Suzi Fenton

FIRST EDITION
ISBN 0-06-270247-5
ISBN 0-06-273686-8 (paper)

The Library of Congress information available upon request.

01 02 03 04 RRD 10

To the Clients of Edelman Financial Services Inc.
I am privileged to be associated with these fine people,
for they truly are the backbone of America.
Being permitted to serve them is the greatest honor.

Table of Contents

Secret #4

Mind Over Money

Secret #5

Secret #6

Secret #7

Secret #8

In Their Own Words

Afterthoughts

About the Author

Index

Acknowledgements

A book of this type is the result of extensive research efforts of a great many people. I am indebted to those among my staff who interviewed hundreds of our clients for this project. These staffers include Marsha Argent, Rodel Berber, Jennie Blinick, Stacy Brosnahan, Peggy Butler, Will Casserly, Brandon Corso, Renee West, Stacy Duffy, Jean Edelman, John Faeth, Suzi Fenton, Kathy Freese, Edward Gekosky, Mike Gifford, Nancy Hale, Susan Harpe, Teresa Harrington, Gwen Hill, Marie Johnson, Mark Katzenberger, Pam Kelly, Lisa Korhnak, Bruce Mattare, John McCoy, Angela McGlawn, Tamara Milwee, Monica Morehouse, Fran Norris, Kathy Renzetti, Carol Roberts, Lesley Roberts, Evy Sheehan, Catherine Smith, Mary Jane Spradlin, Susan Theofanidis, Dale Tison, Mike Volpe, Rosa Zediker, and Denise Zuchelli.

I am especially indebted to Lisa Korhnak and her team, which consisted of Renee West, Bruce Mattare, Kathy Renzetti, Mike Volpe, and Rosa Zediker. The results of their extensive, in-depth follow-up client interviews are displayed throughout the book.

Many thanks also to Sid Groenemann and his colleagues at Market Facts, Inc. They were a pleasure to work with and handled their assignment with great skill, grace, and professionalism—and on remarkably short notice. Their reputation as one of the nation's premier survey research firms is well deserved.

I also gratefully acknowledge the contributions of my fellow financial planners at Edelman Financial Services Inc., including Jack Bubon, CFP, Ed Moore, CFP, Cindee Berar, MBA, RFC, Jan Kowal, CPA, CFP, Kris Duwar, Diane Jensen, CFP, Betty O'Lear, CFP, Doug Rabil, CFP, Andrew Massaro, CFP, Joe Gilmore, RFC, and Kelsey Williams, RFC. I am lucky to have them.

Thanks also to Adrian Reilly for his artwork, Suzi Fenton for her layout and design, my agent Gail Ross, and to the folks at HarperCollins, especially my editor Robert Wilson.

And most of all, many, many heartfelt thanks to the thousands of clients who agreed to share intimate details of their financial lives. Without their selfless contributions, this book would not have been possible.

Introduction

This book is unlike any personal finance book you've ever seen. True, like some other books, it shows you how successful people got that way. But unlike other books, this one does not focus on the super-elite of Wall Street or neighbors of yours who own successful businesses. Instead, you'll get to know ordinary Americans—people just like you—who have somehow managed to accumulate wealth despite the fact that they never earned all that much money or achieved the highest levels in business, politics, or the arts.

Instead, these people are middle- and upper-middle-class citizens. They are schoolteachers, engineers, government employees, computer analysts, lawyers, physical therapists, office managers, doctors, journalists, graphic designers, and musicians. They are your neighbors, co-workers, friends, and relatives. And they are similar to you in age and marital status, with similar incomes and expenses, with kids and pets—and with similar goals and aspirations. Like you, they want a comfortable home in a quiet neighborhood, kids who get through college, marry and have children of their own, and they want to have enough money left over to care for their elderly parents while retaining enough to feel secure during their own retirement.

But unlike most others, these ordinary Americans have done something extraordinary: they somehow have managed to achieve all of these goals, while accumulating enough money to be able to live out their lives in comfort and financial security.

How did they do it?

The pages that follow give you the answer. You'll discover the actual real-life practices and habits of my firm's 5,000 clients. So it won't be me who's guiding you in these pages; it'll be the wonderful message-filled stories of ordinary Americans who have achieved extraordinary success.

As the owner of one of the largest financial planning and investment management firms in the nation, I have clients who (naturally) tend to be financially successful. But my colleagues and I have had very little to do with it, and this is not a chicken-and-egg question. The consumers who hire my firm do so because they are successful, not the other way around. Successful people—and those who want to be—are the kind of people who hire financial advisors. I didn't make them rich, nor does any financial advisor make a person rich. Our clients either are rich by the time they hire us, or they will become rich anyway, because that is their nature. I simply have been fortunate enough to enjoy their journey with them. Indeed, I am convinced that even if they hired some other financial planning firm, they still (in most cases!) would have achieved similar success. After all, the person who joins a health club is the kind of person who is—or will be—physically fit. Which health club she joins has much less impact on her results.

Therefore, all of my firm's clients are members of a self-appointed group: a group of successful investors. Consequently, they have many habits and traits in common. To write this book, all I had to do was discover what those traits are, and reveal them here for your benefit.

I accomplished this goal in a rather obvious way: I simply asked some of my firm's clients how they did it (okay, I asked about four thousand of them). Market Facts, the prestigious survey research firm, issued, collected, tabulated, and analyzed the results of an extensive eight-page survey I wrote. These questions asked my clients how they've handled money throughout their lives, and I searched their answers for commonality, consistency, and replicability.

Did we discover clear patterns and trends among this diverse group of people? Yes, we did. Poring through the data, I identified eight major themes that were common to nearly everyone who responded to the survey. Each of these themes, in my opinion, reflects the biggest factors influencing my clients' ability to produce the wealth they now have. And the best news: anyone can easily duplicate these themes in their own life.

That means you, too, can achieve financial success as easily and as surely as they did. You can do it without having to undergo major upheavals in your life. You don't need to quit your job and open a convenience store. You don't need to become a day-trader, spending your life staring at a computer screen while yelling orders into the phone at some broker. You don't have to subscribe to dozens of personal finance magazines or religiously tune in to *Rukeyser,* subject yourself to intense behavior modification, connect with your inner self, or resolve all those conflicts with your mother. Nor do you have to invent some revolutionary gizmo that will change the world. All you need to do is follow eight simple financial strategies. You'll discover that they are remarkably easy to implement and remarkably effective. All of my clients have achieved (or are in the process of achieving) financial success, and there's not a Warren Buffett or Bill Gates in the crowd. Just like my clients, you can do it, too!

As you read this book, prepare to be surprised. The strategies you're about to explore are not what you might expect, and in fact, they may seem counterintuitive. Keep an open mind.

Expect to see yourself—in two ways. First, through the many stories my clients will share with you, you'll see that you're not very different from them, and this will show you that you can do what they did. Second, after examining their experiences, you're likely to exclaim, "Uh oh! I'm doing the opposite of what they did!"

And finally, expect to get excited. You'll discover how easy it is to stop doing what you've been doing wrong and start doing what you need to do, so you, too, can achieve financial success. Not only is the list remarkably short, but the actions required are so simple that anyone can do it—including you. The success stories of my firm's clients will empower you, and you'll love how that makes you feel.

Ric Edelman
November 1999

Do You Want to Be Like These People?

Before we examine the financial strategies my clients used to become successful, let's first make sure you want to be like them. After all, if their level of success doesn't match your description of success, there's little point in learning how they did it.

The average age of the clients we surveyed is 57. Therefore, by the time you are 57, would you like to:

- Own a quarter-million dollar home?

- Have nearly half-a-million dollars in savings and investments?

- Have a total annual household income of $120,000?

If you would consider yourself "wealthy" to attain this level of wealth, keep reading. My clients will show you how to achieve it.

SECRET #1

They Carry a Mortgage on Their Homes Even Though They Can Afford to Pay it Off.

SECRET #1
They Carry a Mortgage on Their Homes Even Though They Can Afford to Pay it Off.

If you had enough money to pay off your mortgage right now, would you?

Many people would. In fact, "The American Dream" is to own your home—and to own it outright, with no mortgage. Imagine owning your home without having to send a check to a mortgage company or bank every month! Being so fortunate must evoke such a sense of security, satisfaction, and well-being that you could only dream of it! Imagine the feeling you'll enjoy when, after 30 long years—360 monthly payments—you finally make your last payment, and the house is yours forever!

If The American Dream is so wonderful, how can you explain the fact that thousands of financially successful people—people who have more than enough money to pay off their mortgage right now—refuse to do so?

Consider these facts derived from my survey research. Of the respondents:

1. The average home value is $255,700; the average mortgage balance is $142,000. Even though 100% have the ability to own their home without a mortgage, 83% carry a mortgage anyway.

2. 100% have the ability to send in extra money along with their monthly payments, to eliminate the mortgage ahead of schedule—but 90% choose not to. Instead, 85% of the respondents have a 30-year loan and no one in this group sends in extra principal payments or participates in bi-weekly mortgage plans.

Clearly, these successful Americans are not bothered by carrying a big, long mortgage. Compare yourself to them. If you have a mortgage and are struggling to pay it off, or if you're dreaming of the day when you make your final payment, you're trying to do something that financially successful people do not do.

What do they know that you don't?

It's vital that you understand what's happening here. And we begin with the fact that talking about mortgages is not a conversation about economics or finance.

It's about emotions.

You "love" the idea of owning your own home. You "hate" your mortgage. If you're like many, you may even "fear" it. All of these are emotional words; none of them are financial. Yet, a mortgage is a financial tool—not an emotional state of mind.

Why, then, do you feel the way you do about your mortgage?

Blame it on your parents.[1]

Just about everything you've learned about money, you've learned from your parents. Even though Mom and Dad never said a word to you about money, they had lots to say about mortgages—especially when you announced you were planning to buy your first house. "Make a big down payment," they told you, "and keep the mortgage payment low." "Pay it off early, child. You don't want that mortgage hanging over your head."

Indeed, your parents and grandparents made it very clear to you that mortgages are bad, something to minimize, or to avoid whenever possible. A necessary evil at best. But what they never told you was why they felt this way about mortgages. It's important you understand their perspective or you'll fail to understand why their advice is bad for you. So let's look at mortgages from your parents' and grandparents' point of view.

---

[1] Cool!

Why People Fear Mortgages—and Why You Shouldn't

Our story begins in the 1920s. Back then, houses typically cost $5,000. Sure doesn't sound like much, until you consider that the average annual income in the U.S. was $1,434 in 1925. Consequently, few people could afford to pay cash for their homes—just like today. So, people borrowed the money from banks—again, just like today. But the loans were structured differently back then. A common clause in the loan agreement gave banks the right to demand full repayment of the loan at any time; if you failed to repay your loan when asked, the bank had the right to take your house from you and sell it to recoup its money.

So although the terms called for you to send $24 to the bank every month[2] to pay off that $4,500 balance over 30 years, you knew you suddenly might be required to repay the remaining balance in full at any time. You didn't worry about that clause, because you knew that having the bank ask you for $4,500 in cash, well, they might as well ask for the moon.

Then came October 29, 1929.

When the stock market crashed, millions of investors lost huge sums of money. Problem was, it wasn't their money they had lost. You see, most investors back then had bought stocks with borrowed money—money lent to them by their stockbrokers, called a "margin account."[3] Under rules then in effect, you were allowed to buy $100 worth of stock by giving your broker just ten bucks; your broker would loan you the other $90. So when the Crash hit, knocking 30% off the value of everyone's stock portfolios, a typical brokerage account that previously was worth $100 now contained stocks worth only $70. But the investor had borrowed $90 to buy them! This led to a "margin call," where the broker would tell the investor that because his account had exceeded the "margin limits, " he had to come up with more cash. If the investor failed to do so, the broker would

---

[2] Wow!

[3] So-called because brokers would make a note in the margin of their trade blotters that the client had borrowed money to buy the stocks.

begin to sell some of the investor's stocks, and the broker would continue selling until enough cash was raised to meet the margin call.

Selling off the portfolio was the last thing the investor wanted his broker to do. The stocks were already down 30%—this was the worst time to sell. So, to avoid the margin call, the investor went to his bank and withdrew enough cash to meet his broker's margin call. The investor had to act quickly, because under stock exchange rules, margin calls must be fulfilled within 24 hours. Therefore, in the days following the Crash of '29, a lot of investors went to their banks and made withdrawals.

It didn't take long for the banks to run out of cash.

When they did, word quickly spread. Bank depositors stampeded the banks, demanding their money. To get more, the banks started calling their loans due. They sent telegrams to their borrowers, demanding they pay off their loans immediately and in full. Because these homeowners didn't have the cash—you might as well ask for the moon—the banks foreclosed and put the houses up for sale in a desperate attempt to raise capital.

It didn't work.

With no one willing or able to buy the houses, banks found themselves owning virtually worthless real estate. Unable to satisfy depositors who were demanding their cash, the banks closed their doors, many of them never to reopen. With investors unable to get their cash from their banks, they were unable to meet their margin calls—so their brokers started selling out their holdings. But everyone was in this dilemma, so the brokers couldn't find buyers for the stocks. With no one willing to buy, the brokers had to continually drop the stocks' prices.

Ultimately, the Great Depression saw the stock market fall more than 75% from its 1929 highs. More than half of the nation's banks failed. Tens of millions of Americans lost their jobs as companies went bankrupt. And millions of homeowners, unable to raise the cash they needed to pay off their loans, lost their homes. The American Dream had become a national nightmare.

But not for those who owned their homes outright. These lucky few were immune to the banks' collapse. With no loans to repay, they got no telegram demanding full payment. As their neighbors went broke and lost their homes, with thousands committing suicide, those who owned their homes outright succeeded in keeping them. They might not have found work, or had much to eat, but they kept a roof over their children's heads.

And thus was born America's mantra: Always own your home outright. Never carry a mortgage.

And yet, despite all this, a small group of Americans insist on carrying a mortgage even when they can afford not to. Why would they place themselves at such risk? Don't they know what they're doing?

Actually, they know exactly what they're doing. They are among America's elite: the wealthiest 1% of the population. Not only do they know what they're doing, they know why they're doing it. It's *you* who fails to understand.

What you and your parents have failed to realize is that our nation has learned from the harsh lessons of the 1930s. A '30s-like depression has not been repeated, and indeed cannot occur again, because of the safeguards that have long since been put into place.[4] Among them:

1) Banks are no longer able to cancel your mortgage. This means that if you have a mortgage, there is no risk that you suddenly might be required to pay off the loan. Instead, provided you make each month's payment on time, no bank can force you to pay off the entire remaining balance.

---

[4] This is not to say that a Depression can't occur again—merely that a "'30s-like Depression" can't occur again. The next time financial disaster strikes, the causes will be vastly different.

2) Customers are no longer permitted to buy stocks with only 10% down. The maximum margin limit is 50%; for some securities it's 20%—and zero for speculative investments (such as internet stocks). This dramatically reduces (or even eliminates) the risk that an investor will get a margin call, which in turn reduces the risk that investors will need to make simultaneous and massive withdrawal demands on their banks due to cash flow problems in the stock market.

3) By similar action, the Glass-Steagall Act of 1933 kicked banks out of the stock underwriting business. By building a "Chinese Wall" between Wall Street and the banking business, the government insured that brokerage failures wouldn't harm the banking business.

4) Congress created the Federal Deposit Insurance Corporation in 1933 to protect consumers from future bank failures. Before FDIC, consumers were unprotected in the event their bank went broke because of bad lending practices. Today, however, consumer accounts up to $100,000 are protected, giving citizens a level of confidence in banks that didn't exist in the 1920s and early 1930s. Congress also created similar programs for savings & loans (FSLIC, now part of FDIC), credit unions (NCUSIF) and pension funds (Pension Benefits Guaranty Corporation). Though rare, bank failures still occur, but no depositor has ever lost his or her life savings as a result of one, thanks to these programs.[5]

5) The Federal Reserve, which controls the nation's money supply, now understands that the best way to prevent a "run on the bank" is to provide banks with all the cash

---

[5] Don't assume the presence of FDIC means banks are perfectly safe, though. Still unknown is what would happen in the event of a system-wide banking collapse. However, occasional bank failures are no longer a risk for consumers (though they could be for taxpayers, as the S&L crisis of the 1980s proved!)

they need, rather than withhold currency like the government did in 1929. Back then, the government feared that flooding the banks with cash would result in inflation. Instead, the government created the worst depression in history. But we've learned our lesson, as shown by two modern examples:

a) Within hours of the Crash of 1987 (the first 1929-like crash since, well, 1929), Fed Chairman Alan Greenspan announced that the Federal Reserve would supply as much cash to the nation's banks as they needed—reassuring all Americans (and the world) that there would be no repeat of 1929. Greenspan's comments are widely credited with calming much of the panic on that October 19th, and many argue that his actions, more than any other, helped America avoid another depression.

b) Responding to concerns that computer problems would lead to bank failures in the year 2000, the government said it would it print and distribute $200 billion in extra currency, so that banks would have more than enough cash on hand to meet any withdrawal request—even if the computers stopped working.

6) Competition in the mortgage industry has dramatically increased. If one lender won't provide you the loan you seek, odds are better than ever that another will. And new, innovative loan programs make mortgages more affordable than ever—reducing the likelihood that you'll default.

The point? Those who tell you to pay off your mortgage are basing their advice on *their fear*—fear that having a mortgage might cause you to lose your home. But as you now understand, your risks of losing your home are negligible compared to homeowners of the 1920s. And that means these fears are largely unfounded.

Largely, but not completely. Because there are still two aspects of mortgages that I haven't yet dispelled for you: the challenge of affording the monthly payment and the interest you'll save by not having to make that payment.

Let's start with the first one. Do you fear that you might not be able to make the payment every month? This is a problem, because, as I pointed out, the bank *can* foreclose on your home if you fail to make your monthly payment on time. Therefore, you fear, what if you suddenly lose your job? With no income, you won't be able to make the payments—and you'll lose your house.

Isn't this enough of a reason to eliminate your mortgage? No.[6]

The truth is that the less money you have, and the more worried you are that you might lose your job, the more important it is that you keep a big mortgage. This might seem counterintuitive (as I warned you in the introduction), but it's the truth. And it's critical that you understand this point. Bill Gates can choose to have or not have a mortgage; it won't make much difference in his life either way. But if you have little money and even less job security, having a mortgage is the *safest* way to handle your home.

Why? Because there's more to life than having a home. Like putting food on the table.

Let me give you an example, adapted from my second book, *The New Rules of Money*[7]. Karen and Janet each earn $35,000 a year. Both are in the 28% tax bracket. Both have $12,000 in savings. Each buys a $120,000 house.

Janet wants to minimize her mortgage, so she uses her $12,000 in savings as a down payment, and opts for a 15-year loan at 6.5%. Her monthly payment is $941, but only 57% of that payment is tax-deductible interest; the rest is principal. Therefore, Janet's net after-tax cost for her mortgage is $790. And to pay off her mortgage even quicker, Janet sends in an

---

[6] But nice try.
[7] At bookstores everywhere!

extra $50 with every payment. Of course, these payments are devoted entirely to principal, and therefore provide no tax deduction.

Karen, on the other hand, obtains a 30-year mortgage at 7%, putting down just $6,000 and financing the rest. Even though her mortgage balance is bigger than Janet's ($114,000 compared to $108,000), her monthly payment is just $758. That's not all: Because 81% of the payment is interest, Karen's after-tax cost is just $586 a month—$204 less than what Janet pays! Karen invests these savings each month for five years, earning 8% after taxes per year. And where Janet sends to her lender an extra $50 each month, Karen adds $50 to her savings. Result: Over five years, Karen accumulates a total of $12,675.

Suddenly, both women find themselves out of work. Because Janet used all her money as a down payment, she has no savings to rely on. True, she's got $43,285 worth of equity in her house (because she started with a big down payment and has been making monthly payments ever since), but that won't help her buy groceries. Being unemployed, she can't refinance, and news of her being out of work caused her bank to reject her application for a home equity line of credit. If she wants to get ahold of her equity, there's only one way for her to do it: She must sell her house. This would force her to lose her home—the one thing she wanted to avoid!

Indeed, Janet has discovered the biggest secret about home-ownership: Your mortgage is a loan against your income; it is not a loan against the value of the house. With no income, you cannot borrow against your equity. Janet better get a job—and quick! Not only can't she afford to buy food, she's about to lose her house!

Karen, by contrast, has little to worry about. With $12,675 in savings, she's easily able to make her payments each month, even without a job. In fact, she's got enough money to make her monthly mortgage payment for nearly two years!

How ironic: Janet didn't want a big mortgage and did everything she could to pay it off quickly. Now, she's discovering that this strategy—rather than safeguarding her home—might cause her to lose it!

Clearly, then, you should not give the bank or builder a large down payment, nor should you be in a hurry to pay off your mortgage. And the less money you have, and the less stable your income, the more important the idea of carrying a big, long mortgage is for you.

But still, there must be something more to this notion of carrying a big, long mortgage. While it's true that fear might lead some people to avoid mortgages, *lack of fear* is not enough to explain why people carry mortgages. No, there must be some other motivator.

And there is. It's called a desire to accumulate wealth.

Here's an important lesson all wealth-wanna-bes must understand: *No one ever got rich by saving money.* Or, put another way, *paying off debt* is not the same as *accumulating assets.*

I stress this because many people think they will be better off financially if they eliminate their mortgage. But this is not true.

"Not true?!" you say. "Of course it is! If I don't have to make a monthly mortgage payment, I'm in far better shape than the guy who has a mortgage!"

I'm sorry, but despite the fact that millions of Americans believe this to be true, such thinking is misguided. You need to know why.

There are two kinds of people who hate mortgages: those who fear them and those who believe that mortgages cost you huge amounts of money in interest charges. We've already resolved the former issue—that *fear* thing—so let me dispel the myths surrounding the latter.

Why People Hate Mortgages—and Why You Shouldn't

Carrying a mortgage doesn't cause you to lose any money at all. In fact, just the opposite is true: carrying a mortgage is actually quite profitable. It's *eliminating the mortgage* that forces you to give up profitable opportunities.

You see, this second group of people—the ones who hate rather than fear mortgages—feel that way because they know, over the life of a 30-year loan, they will spend more in interest than the house cost in the first place. Take Karen, for example. By going with a 30-year loan, she'll spend nearly $159,000 in interest—on a house that cost her only $120,000! This fact drives homeowners nuts. And I mean that sincerely: in order to avoid spending so much money in interest charges, people will do certifiably crazy things. Things like making bigger down payments, choosing 15-year loans, making extra principal payments, and signing up for bi-weekly loan programs. All these things are crazy.[8]

Yet you do these things because you want to save money in interest. For some reason, you have equated *saving money* with *making money*. Yet, the two are *not* synonymous—and you need to learn this right now (because the sooner, the better). You see, what you've done is something psychologists call *compartmentalization*.[9] It's found in the science of heuristics, used in the new field of behavioral finance (the study of why people do with their money what they do). Through compartmentalization, or what I call "Farming vs. Foresting" (which we'll explore more in depth later) you fail to examine the big picture when you make financial decisions. Instead, you focus on a single issue, resolve it, then move on to the next issue. As a result, you make a series of bad financial decisions instead of one good one.

This psychological phenomenon manifests itself clearly in the mortgage decision. You want to save money in interest, so to minimize your costs, you do all the things I described two paragraphs up. With that issue resolved, you then start to focus on saving for retirement, and you do your best to save regularly. As a result, you fail to accumulate wealth—and you can't figure out why.

---

[8] And I mean this literally. We'll introduce the word psychologists use to describe the illness in a moment, but for now, we'll just call people who think this way "wacko."
[9] There's the word!

The reason is simple, though often not clear by any means. By tackling the mortgage issue first, and savings goals second, you fail to consider the role that a mortgage plays in your savings efforts. Your battle to reduce interest expenses is won, but the wealth accumulation war is lost.

Here's why: You know that by reducing the mortgage payment, or even paying off the mortgage completely, you save lots of money in interest charges. While that is correct, you are ignoring another, equally critical fact: Every dollar you give the bank is a dollar you did not invest.

This is a vital point. Mortgages today cost 6.5% to 7.5%. Over the next 30 years, on an average annual basis, will your investments earn at least that much? Absolutely. Even long-term government bonds pay nearly that amount, and stocks have been averaging 11.2% since 1926. But giving your money to the bank to avoid a 7% interest charge denies yourself the opportunity to invest that money where it might earn 10%. Thus, by compartmentalizing, you save 7%—but you lose the chance to earn 10%. Thus, rather than saving you money, getting rid of a mortgage actually costs you 3% per year! Thus, by looking at individual trees, you fail to see the forest.

The irony is that some people feel they are making a good "investment" by paying off their home loan. In fact, all they're doing is burying money under a mattress; they aren't investing it at all. Why? Because your home will grow in value over the next 30 years whether you have a mortgage or not. Think about it. When you sell your house, does any buyer care what your mortgage balance is? Of course not. Neither does the IRS when you calculate your taxable gain or loss. The simple truth is that mortgages do not affect home values.

Therefore, you have a choice. You can pay cash to buy a $200,000 house, enabling you to own it outright, or you can buy that house with 20% down. Let's explore each of these scenarios in detail and see which is better at helping you achieve your true goal—accumulating wealth.

Julia just received $200,000 from the sale of her prior house. Or maybe she exercised some stock options, or got an inheritance, or received an insurance settlement. It doesn't matter where the money came from. The point is, she's loaded—and she wants to buy a new home which costs $200,000. Julia pays cash for the house. This takes all her cash, but it lets her avoid mortgage payments. In 30 years, her house will be worth $600,000, assuming it grows at the rate of 3.5% per year. Pretty smart, she figures.

But Jean takes a different approach. Jean too has $200,000 in cash. Like Julia, Jean also wants to buy a $200,000 house. But Jean puts down only 20%, or $40,000, obtaining a $160,000 mortgage. The monthly payment is $1,064, but it really costs Jean less than that because the mortgage interest is tax-deductible (something Julia failed to consider)[10], and the tax savings reduce her monthly mortgage bill by $240, making her net payment just $824 per month. To help her make those monthly payments, Jean invests the $160,000 she didn't give the bank, and earns 10% per year on her money. She's got to pay taxes on those profits, and she does so—but at the 20% long-term capital gains rate, not the 28% ordinary income tax rate.[11] Thus, Jean earns a monthly after-tax return of $1,067. After paying for the loan, she's got $243 per month left over, which she reinvests. After 30 years, Jean (like Julia) has a house worth $600,000 (and, like Julia, it's fully paid for by then). And that's not all. Jean also still has her $160,000—as well as another $550,000 from investing $243 per month over 30 years.

---

[10] Due, again, to compartmentalization. Getting a mortgage is one thing, Julia figures, tax preparation is another—so she fails to consider both issues simultaneously, to her detriment.
[11] This saves another 8%—because while Jean *pays taxes* at the 20% rate, she *saves taxes* at the 28% rate!

Julia wanted to avoid the expenses of a mortgage. Jean wanted to accumulate wealth—and if doing so meant carrying a mortgage, Jean was willing to do it. The result? Jean's net worth is $1,310,000—more than twice as much as Julia's![12]

So don't fret about all the interest the loan is costing you. Focus instead on all the money you're able to save as a result of not giving all your money to the bank in the first place.

But if this monthly payment is still bothering you, let's do some time travelling. You'll see how much fun it is to carry a mortgage.[13] Thirty years ago, in 1970, homes cost an average of $23,400 and 30-year fixed-rate mortgages were 6%. The monthly payment, assuming no money down: $140. That's probably less than your current car payment!

Before you long for the good 'ole days, remember that the average monthly income in America back then was $646. In other words, that $140 mortgage was as challenging to people then as your $1,000 payment is to you. And in 20 years, you'll be teasing your kids[14] about your "low" payment—because incomes and housing prices will be much higher in the future, just as today's wages and prices are much higher than those of 1970!

Indeed, it's important to remember that mortgage payments get cheaper over time, even though they never actually change, because the payments are fixed, while your income grows. So don't fret about having to make that "big" mortgage payment. It won't seem big forever.

For all these reasons, the 30-year mortgage is better than one that you pay off in just 15 years. It also explains why bi-weekly mortgage plans are not great ideas. You see, both those programs merely cause you to pay more in principal each year

---

[12] Some readers will be unconvinced by this example. They will claim that Julia can invest $824 per month more than Jean, because Jean is making a mortgage payment that Julia has avoided, and that this advantage will enable Julia to accumulate more money than Jean over 30 years. Sorry, but that's not true. Even though Julia can invest $824 per month, Jean gets to invest $160,000 *right now*. And the results: By investing $824 per month at 10% per year for 30 years, Julia would have $1.86 million. But by investing $160,000 today for the next 30 years, also at 10% per year, Jean will have $3.17 million—far more than Julia. No matter how you handle it, carrying a mortgage enables you to produce greater wealth.

[13] Yes, fun!

[14] Now, isn't that fun?

than you do with a 30-year loan. And the more you pay in principal, the quicker you pay off your loan. But as we've seen, giving the bank any more principal than necessary is the last thing you want to do, because:

1) You get no tax break when giving the bank principal. You save on taxes only when you pay interest.

2) Money you invest is taxed at a lower rate than what you save in tax-deductible interest. Therefore, you want to maximize your interest payment while minimizing your principal payment.

3) Money you give to the bank is money you'll never see again—unless you refinance. If you think this notion is absurdly obvious, you haven't come across any of the thousands of consumers who tell me that the reason they're hurrying to pay off their mortgages is so they'll be able to borrow against the equity later (read: get a new mortgage) to pay their kids' college tuition bills. Talk about a bizarre strategy! These folks are struggling to give the bank all their money now merely so they can borrow it in the future! Why don't they just invest their cash so that it earns competitive returns and remains available for use whenever needed?

And the most important reason you don't want to give the bank any more money than necessary? Because Cash Is King. Having a home fully paid for is one thing, but being able to cover that unexpected medical expense is another. You'll need cash to pay for a family member's wedding, or to send a kid to college, or just bail someone out of jail. If you lose your job, not owing the bank any money on your house will be of small consolation when they repossess your car because you're house-rich and cash-poor.

And if nothing else convinces you, consider this: the clients of my firm are among the most financially successful of all Americans. They carry a mortgage. If you want to build wealth like they do, it's time you start managing your money the way they do. Starting with your mortgage.

Successful Investors:

They Carry a Mortgage on Their Homes Even Though They Can Afford to Pay it Off.

"In Their Own Words"

We were in the Air Force for almost 30 years, and my wife and I have owned several homes over the past 20 years. We have always had a mortgage. Of course, there were many years when we were so poor we couldn't afford to accelerate mortgage payments even if we wanted to, and later, when we did have the cash, we didn't double down on mortgage payments because we knew that was not where to put our money. Having a mortgage never made us feel uncomfortable. We just always considered it the cost of owning a home. We would encourage others today to get as long a mortgage as they can. Using someone else's money is always better than using your own.

Would I do it again if I could? Absolutely. But I'd do one thing differently: I used to fall into the lap of the Realtor and go with any mortgage available . . . I don't think I shopped around for the best rates in the early days, and looking back, I might have gotten a better deal had I done so.

Michael F. Burke, retired from Air Force, now working as a defense analyst with a large technical corporation. Raised in Saratoga Springs, New York

Elinor K. Burke, former the Air Force nurse, now a printmaker. Raised in Springfield, Massachusetts

Having a mortgage doesn't bother me. I figure it is a good thing; I'm building equity in the home over time as the house grows in value, and in the meantime it gives me a tax advantage, and I retain more control over my spending.

I would encourage younger people today to buy a house, discourage them from buying a condo or townhouse. I agree with the philosophy of having a long mortgage within reason . . . I think ideally if you can put enough down to avoid Private Mortgage Insurance, and can do it without strapping yourself financially, do it.

Jackie Peluso, federal government employee. Divorced. Raised in Rockville, Maryland

---

I've owned homes for 32 years and have always had a mortgage. I did not pay it off early, primarily because of the benefits of being able to deduct the interest from my taxes. Every time we moved to a new home we took out a big mortgage. It was uncomfortable but I felt I was in my prime earning years, so it wouldn't be a long-term burden. I'd advise others to get as big a mortgage as you can afford because over time it provides a tremendous financial benefit.

David Webb, executive with a gas industry research organization. Raised in Lubbock, Texas

Jean Webb, homemaker. Raised in Arab, Alabama

When I bought my first house, I was worried about the payments. But everyone has that same worry. So even though I had anxiety in the beginning, I got acclimated to it.

Charles Canard, retired. Widowed. Raised in Warrenton, Virginia

I always refinanced the house to get out as much equity as I could, mostly because this gave me the cash I needed to open my own business. I'd advise others to buy a house as soon as possible because the future equity is yours. You also build up a good credit record and you get a tax write-off.

Heinrich Hofmann, caterer. Raised in Persenbeug, Austria

Anna R. Hofmann, caterer. Raised in Minas Gerais, Brazil

I was never uncomfortable about my mortgage because I was confident I could make the payments. For investment purposes and the tax write off, it's a good deal. You should get as long a mortgage as you can—and get one you can afford. Once, I paid too much down (on a previous home), and I didn't have enough money to do repairs after that, and so I had to take out a loan. I should have kept my cash in the first place. It would have been cheaper and easier.

Marty C., secretary. Raised in McAlester, Oklahoma

We carry a mortgage because we wanted to put more money into savings. My mother gave us enough money to pay off the house, but we put that money into savings and investing instead. I don't like owing money, but I realized that there are trade-offs in having a mortgage.

My advice: Don't buy as expensive a house as you can afford, but get a big mortgage on the house you do buy. That way, you can live under your income and have money left over for emergencies and savings.

Bea Blacklow, epidemiologist. Raised in Elmont, Long Island

Roger Blacklow, political coordinator. Raised in Washington, DC

When you sign up for a big mortgage, you feel a little buyer's remorse for a while, but you get over it. Even if you think you can't afford it, after you get over the buyer's remorse, you find out it is easier to afford than you realized. So, it's best to go ahead and do it. If I had the chance, I'd go back in time and refinance my mortgage sooner.

Stephanie Thomas, information officer at the U.S. Department of Agriculture. Raised in Springfield, Virginia

Brad Thomas, computer analyst. Raised in Vienna, Virginia

My parents paid cash for their house in 1942. They paid $2,500 and bought two homes on the same lot. My father was an immigrant from Italy, a coal miner, and he saved the money for the purchase. It was a very different world than we live in today. My parents did not talk with me about mortgages. They were from the old country.

The only time I did feel uncomfortable was when I bought my first home in 1967. I really had to pinch pennies to meet the payments and I even took a part-time job for awhile. I had three young children and doctor bills. But my income soon started growing. Before too long, I was okay.

Tony D'Alessandro, electronic engineer. Raised in Wyoming, Pennsylvania

Ruth D'Alessandro, homemaker. Raised in Ayer, Massachusetts

I was never uncomfortable with a mortgage. I was gifted money as a child and I was aware of investing in the stock market as a teenager. Owning a home with a mortgage is like an investment that allows you to get tax benefits.

Pat Black, computer programmer. Raised in Baltimore, Maryland

I have not paid off my mortgage because it is very inexpensive money, plus I get a tax deduction. I've never felt uncomfortable with it, because I was always able to make the payments. And I figured I could always work something out with the bank. I think it's good to carry a mortgage because it's the least expensive money you can find.

Willis H. Martin, systems engineer. Raised in New Freedom, Pennsylvania

Marcia G. Martin, travel agent. Raised in York, Pennsylvania

My parents never talked with me about mortgages because it was a different era. When I was growing up in the '50s, my father made $3 an hour in a steel mill. When we bought our first house in 1976, and I told my dad the purchase price was $50,000—remember, he was born in the early 1900s—he just about had a fit. Being of a different era, going through the depression, he and my mother couldn't understand.

The mortgage is only the first part of owning a home. The maintenance and upkeep are important, too. Be prepared for contingencies and have money for the plumbing, heating, roof repairs, etc. The mortgage is only one part of monthly home expenses.

Bill Harper, retail manager. Raised in McKeesport, Pennsylvania

Shirley Harper, executive secretary. Raised in Front Royal, Virginia

---

I have a mortgage because the interest rate is low—7⅜%— and my feeling is that I make more money in investments and still enjoy tax breaks.

Charles Hottel, computer specialist. Raised in Suitland, Maryland

I have a mortgage because I know that my money can do more for me in the marketplace than by paying off the mortgage early. But when we first signed our life away and saw those huge numbers, and what we were responsible for, I was nervous. But, after you make some payments and you realize it's not any different than paying rent, you get used to it.

The big thing is not to own more house than you can afford. I have friends who have expensive homes that prevent them from having flexibility in their lives.

Name withheld, business consultant. Raised in Tempe, Arizona

Spouse, physician. Raised in Tulsa, Oklahoma

We've been homeowners for 39 years and have always had a mortgage. In the earlier years, we didn't have the money to pay it off, and now we realize there's no reason to. Our parents didn't pay off their mortgage early, either. They used their money for other things.

When we bought our first home, we paid $19,000 for it, and after signing the papers, we looked at each other and said, "What have we done!" We didn't even have a credit card in those days. We overcame our fears just by spending conservatively.

The trick is to avoid becoming house poor. Stay within the confines of your earning power and don't become dependent on two incomes to afford the mortgage. Put down just enough to buy the house, and invest the rest.

B.A., V.P. of specialty leasing for shopping centers. Raised in Traverse City, Michigan

D.A., field service engineer in an aviation field. Raised in Lansing, Michigan

Paying off a mortgage at a faster rate only benefits the mortgage company. We could invest the additional payments and maintain a tax deduction.

Neil Walp, retired regional economic planner. Raised in Bloomsburg, Pennsylvania

Mary Walp, commercial credit analyst. Raised in Lightstreet, Pennsylvania

The biggest reason we keep our mortgage is for the tax deductions. My parents always wanted me to pay it off, though, because of the security of owning your own home—no one can take it away from you, they felt.

Faye Wood, software engineer. Raised in Elon College, North Carolina

Thomas Wood, procurement executive. Raised in Battle Creek, Michigan

I remember that my parents didn't have a mortgage for very long. Growing up in our neighborhood, there were always celebrations when people paid off their mortgages. They were called "mortgage-burning parties." Paying off the mortgage early was the thing people did. It gave people a sense of security to have a roof over their heads.

When we bought our first house, in the early 1960s, we were overwhelmed with the gigantic debt, and the house was only $20,000! But we never tried to pay it off early. The fact that you paid a little bit each month gave us the same sense of ownership that our parents had, and it let us keep the rest of our money to cover our payments and still be able to pay for other things.

Today, home buying is not an investment. Instead, it's a

place to stay where you can also get a tax advantage. That's why, these days, I think it's better to carry a mortgage and use the extra cash for investments. To pay off your mortgage, you eat up all your cash. But if you have a mortgage, you get tax advantages and you can use the cash for investments. That seems to be the better thing to do today.

Name withheld, federal civil servant, retired

Spouse, retired from military

When I first owned a home I was 20-something, and although my parents didn't teach me about mortgages, I grew up in an environment that abhorred debt. To this day I pay off my credit cards immediately. But, I will never pay off my mortgage. I'd rather take the cash I have and invest it somewhere for a better rate of return. Yet, whenever you assume a big mortgage, you ask yourself, "How am I going to pay for this if I lose my job?" So I use the power of positive thinking.

I used to think of owning a home as an investment, but now I think your home is merely a place where you live. That's why I'd advise people to get the biggest mortgage at the lowest rate possible and invest the rest.

Bill Perrick, salesperson. Raised in Scranton, Pennsylvania

Sandi Perrick, teacher. Raised in Washington, DC

My husband's parents are paying double and triple on their mortgage payments.

It's just something passed down from their parents. We've talked to them about it, but they don't want to carry debt. They are children of parents who were raised in the depression, so there's no changing them. But having a mortgage doesn't bother me. Maybe I'm naive, but I have faith!

The reason it makes sense not to tie up money in a house is because the house is more expensive than you think. It's not just the mortgage, but also maintenance and decorating. It's not so scary if you qualify for the right mortgage.

D.R., advertising sales executive. Raised in Crofton, Maryland

D.R., management consultant. Raised in Crofton, Maryland

---

§§

We've owned a home for 31 years. At first, we had a mortgage because we couldn't afford to pay cash, but now there's no advantage to paying it off because the money's better invested elsewhere.

We were nervous initially, 31 years ago, because it was our first home, and I bought to the maximum extent I could afford. But over time, my earning power went up . . . and as we got raises, the strain became less, and eventually, it wasn't a strain anymore.

I used to believe that real estate was a good investment, but that's not true anymore; now, it's just a place to live. But I still strongly advise others to own a home as opposed to renting.

Jerry White-Partain, systems analyst. Raised in Chatanooga, Tennessee

Camille White-Partain, V.P. of consulting firm. Raised in New York, New York

---

§§

From a budgetary standpoint, I think of the mortgage payment as just coming out of my income each month. It was a bit scary at first, but I just overcame it.

Diana D., software developer. Raised in Fairfax, Virginia

I've owned a home for 39 years. I have a mortgage because I like to have my money working for me; I don't want it all in just the house. Plus I get a tax deduction.

Shirley Pelzel, assistant to general manager. Raised in Pittsburgh, Pennsylvania

---

It doesn't make sense for me to pay off my mortgage because I would lose the tax deduction. I only have a certain amount of money, and to use it all for the mortgage would be at the expense of some better investments.

My parents were from the old school and said mortgages are bad, that I should pay it off as soon as possible. I didn't take their advice, obviously. But when I first got my mortgage, I was really worried ... it seemed like an awful lot of money, especially when you're young. But my income has gone up, and I felt confident over the years.

Stephen Foster, network engineer. Raised in Erlanger, Kentucky

Debbie Foster, H.R. manager. Raised in Vienna, Virginia

The first time we ever got into a mortgage (27 years ago), we were scared to death that we couldn't make the payment, but we've gotten over it and never looked back because we realized we could make it work. By making the repayment period as long as possible, you get the lowest monthly payment, and you can place the rest of your money in other investments.

Paul Richard, defense contractor. Raised in Catonsville, Maryland

Harriet Richard, registered nurse. Raised in Catonsville, Maryland

The mortgage is the only tax deduction we get anymore. It's uncomfortable when you sign on the dotted line at settlement, but you just have to do it.

There's a lot more to owning a home than just the mortgage. My son's in his first year of college, and he and his friends are thinking of buying a home instead of renting one. I told him to think about it carefully . . . he thought you just make payments, but he forgot about things like insurance, repairs, taxes, and the down payment.

There's nothing wrong with carrying a mortgage, as long as it's the only debt you have.

Loni McConchie, administrative assistant. Raised in Easton, Maryland

Michael McConchie. Raised in Washington, DC

SECRET #2

They Don't Diversify the Money They Contribute to Their Employer Retirement Plans.

Instead, They Put All Their Contributions Into One Asset Class—the One Few Others Choose.

SECRET #2

They Don't Diversify the Money They Contribute to Their Employer Retirement Plans.

Instead, They Put All Their Contributions Into One Asset Class—the One Few Others Choose.

Ten years ago, you knew little about investing. You probably didn't even own a mutual fund, let alone know the meaning of NAV.[15] But today, you're much more familiar with investments. You own mutual funds, maybe even some stocks, and you participate in your company's retirement plan.

You once thought that people achieved investment success by somehow managing to buy the "right" funds or the "right" stocks. You thought that way because all your friends and relatives who were into investing kept bragging about the money they made on their last trade. What you didn't realize then (but which you know now) is that they never mentioned their losses, leading you to conclude that they never had any. Today, you know better.

And it wasn't just friends and family who were fooling you. The personal finance press did a number on you, too. They keep issuing cover stories with headlines that scream, "Hot Funds to Buy Now!" and "Six Sizzling Stocks for the Summer!" These headlines give you the impression that (a) your financial success depends on your ability to pick the right stocks or mutual funds and (b) you're too much of a clod to make such picks, so you'd better buy this issue and take our advice instead.

---

[15] Come to think of it, you *still* might not know what that means—even if you *do* own a mutual fund. For the answer, as well as how to pronounce it, turn to footnote 14 on page 167—but not in this book. Look in *The Truth About Money*. How's that for a cheesy way to promote my book? And readers of my second book (see footnote #50 on page 551) will notice the return of footnotes to footnotes. And further note the cheesy promotion of my book.

So you went and read lots of magazines, tuned into lots of radio and TV shows—and followed lots of hot tips. And you never quite got rich. In fact, your investments lost money as often as they made money. Soon, you realized that you weren't going to achieve financial success this way.

But you kept searching and learning, attending seminars and reading books and subscribing to yet more magazines and tuning into more radio and TV talk shows. Eventually, it became a bit more clear. You began to hear some suggest that the key to investment success is *not* picking the right stock, or getting into or out of the market at the right time.[16] Instead, you could achieve success through something called *diversification*. Nobody had ever talked with you about this before—certainly not the personal finance press. And certainly not the gals standing on the floor of the New York Stock Exchange yelling up at the camera, "It's very chaotic here! Fishboon's earnings revision has caused an uptick in cyclicals, and the trin is moving fast!"[17]

Indeed, you've begun to understand diversification. It's The Power of the Force. Like most, your first experience with the Force was with the Dark Side (stock-picking), and consequently, you tried to get rich quick by buying hot stocks and fad funds, all in the hope of making a fortune. It's not that you were greedy.[18] It's just that this is how everyone who's rich got that way—through stock picking and fund fancying.[19] After all, the personal finance press—as well as your neighbors and co-workers—made it very clear to you: investment selection is the key to financial wealth. That must be true, you figured, because it was the only thing anyone ever talked about. You're in a horse race, they implied, and if you failed to pick the right horse—you risked losing everything.

No wonder so many people fear Wall Street.

---

[16] More on that later.

[17] As if (a) that matters and (b) anyone knows what that means.

[18] Well, okay, maybe you were.

[19] Or, at least, that's what you thought.

Why Investment Selection is Part of The Dark Side

It's time you learned the truth. Investment selection has much less to do with achieving wealth than you think. You see, if you really were in a horse race, the horse indeed would have a huge effect on your results. But you're not in a horse race. Instead, you're playing horseshoes. Therefore, you don't need to pick the winner, and it's not a winner-take-all situation. Rather, in a game of horseshoes, as I explained in *The New Rules of Money*[20], merely being close is good enough to win.

You and I are very fortunate that investment selection doesn't matter very much—because it's highly unlikely that either of us will ever pick each year's #1 performer from among 10,000 mutual funds or 7,200 stocks. There are three simple reasons we're not going to achieve wealth by attempting this:

1) You have only one chance in 10,000 to pick the "right" fund. You might as well try to win the lottery.

2) You've got to pick the "right" fund at precisely the "right" time—because the "#1" fund changes every year. This makes the challenge doubly difficult.

3) Even if "your pick" somehow does manage to double in value in a year, big deal! The five grand you invested will now be worth ten grand—and that's hardly enough to retire on. Indeed, the only way to really make a fortune through stock-picking is to:

   a) Invest your entire life savings into *one* stock and hope it becomes the stock of the century. Say you invest $100,000 into one stock (by cashing in all your other investments, putting your watch and wedding ring in hock, and even borrowing from your in-laws) and that stock gains 1,000% in a year (although it's a rare stock that does this, at least one does it every year). If this miracle happened, your

---

[20] On sale now! Just $24.95.

net worth would be one million dollars. Hey, now we're talking! You can sell that stock, net $775,000 or so after state and federal taxes and reinvest the proceeds into T-bills, collecting 6.5% in interest annually. That's roughly $50,000 a year, a tidy sum on which many can retire.

But are you willing to gamble your life savings on one stock in the hopes that it will produce such a return? I doubt it. Therefore, you're not going to accumulate wealth by following Strategy 2(a). So let's try Strategy 2(b):

b) Instead of investing $100,000 into that one stock, let's invest just $1,500. After that stock gains 1,000% in a year, you'll have fifteen grand, or $11,625 after taxes. Reinvest that eleven grand into another stock, have it also grow by 1,000%, and after the second year, you'll net $90,000 after taxes. Split the ninety grand into nine piles of $10,000 each, buy nine more stocks, and let them each gain 1,000% in the third year. You'll have just under $700,000; it's not quite as much as 2(a) produces and this takes three years to accomplish instead of one. Still, when you invest the balance into those T-bills, you'll enjoy an annual income of $45,000 for life. There's only one *teensy weensy* detail required: you must pick *eleven stocks that each gain one thousand percent in a year*. But other than that, this is a sure thing!

Do I *really* have to explain how absurd these ideas are?[21]

It is painfully clear that these strategies are impossible to implement successfully. It also explains why few people are able to "get rich quick" (and why those who do, such as lottery winners, must ascribe their success to sheer luck).

---

[21] Please say no.

Despite the fact that no one accumulates wealth by picking the "right" stocks, many persist in trying, with plenty of encouragement offered by cover stories in the personal finance press and pundits cruising the airwaves with their latest picks. Experienced investors know all this is a sham, so they stay away from horse-picking.

So, if successful investors know they can't pick the right horse, what do they do? Simple: they pick *every* horse. For this truly is how wealth is created, and it is what diversification is all about.

The Power of The Force

As an investment strategy, diversification merely means that you buy many investments, rather than just one or two. Sounds simple enough, but at first blush, it doesn't seem to offer much value. Consider the person who buys five investments. Since he's not a great stock picker, he's lucky to select even one winner. But the same law of averages that prevents him from picking five great investments also prevents him from picking five worthless ones. Therefore, let's say his picks perform as follows after one year:

Results of Investment One	-10%
Results of Investment Two	+ 3%
Results of Investment Three	+ 5%
Results of Investment Four	+ 8%
Results of Investment Five	+12%

Clearly, this guy is not doing a great job at picking investments. He's got one dog, two downright mediocre investments, a fourth that's okay, and only one investment that's managed to earn as much as the long-term average performance of the stock market. And there's no big winner in sight. If he started with $100,000—placing $20,000 into each position—he'd have $103,600 at the end of one year.

Ironically, though, if at the start of that year he had instead put the entire $100,000 into a bank CD, where he'd have earned an easy 5% return, he'd now have $105,000—or $1,400 more than he gets by diversifying. Why? Because the diversified portfolio gained an average of just 3.6%. And it's obvious that 5% beats 3.6%.

The results seem clear: the CD beats diversification, as this one-year example shows. Therefore, we could expect similar results if we conduct the experiment over 10 years. Since 5% always beats 3.6%, the CD will always beat diversification. Won't it?

No.[22]

If we compare these two portfolios after 10 years, assuming the annual returns are the same, we'll discover that the diversified portfolio is worth $171,725, while the CD is worth just $162,889. Over long periods, diversification produced greater wealth than the CD, something it failed to do in the shorter period. But if the average annual returns haven't changed, how can that be?

The answer: the average annual returns *have* changed, but it's difficult to see why at first. To understand what's going on, let's examine most closely the two extreme investments—the one losing the most and the one gaining the most.

Each year, one investment in our portfolio is losing 10%. In the first year, that loser constitutes 20% of the total portfolio—the same "weighting" as the investment that's about to gain 12%. As a result, the loser's impact on the total portfolio is the same as the winner's impact. Result: the average annual total return from the entire portfolio is 3.6%.

But over time, things change. By the beginning of the 10th year, the entire portfolio is worth $160,312. Of this amount, the losing investment is worth only $7,748 (because it has steadily dropped in value over the past nine years), while the winning investment has ballooned to $55,462. In other words, the investment that's about to lose another 10% currently

---

[22] But again, nice try.

represents only 4.8% of the total portfolio, while the investment that's about to gain 12% constitutes 48.3% of the total. Clearly, the winner is contributing more to the results than the loser is taking away, and consequently, the average annual return in this 10th year is 5.6%—or 12% better than the CD, which is stuck earning the same 5% as before.

Thus, over long periods, the diversified portfolio beats the CD, and the more time you give it, the more dramatic its victory.

(Note: before math fanatics cry "foul!" let me point out a couple of things about this example. First, no investment is going to perform identically for 10 straight years, and therefore, it's quite possible that the previous loser—the one worth only seven grand after year nine—could be the one that's about to gain 12% in the 10th year, while the prior winner could be set to become the 10th year's dog. If this were to occur, the loser's positive impact on the portfolio wouldn't be very great, while the prior winner's sudden downfall would be devastating. Fine. I acknowledge that. To which I have four things to say in response: First, each investment within any portfolio will produce it's own average annual return, and it is these figures on which I am relying to demonstrate average consistency per investment over the 10 years, which enables my example to serve as a good teaching tool; second, I covered this point in detail in Rule 42 of my previous book, *The New Rules of Money* [23], and I will do so again a bit further down; third, portfolio rebalancing is a routine part of effective money management, and fourth, *This is just an example. Buzz off.*)

Using The Force

Now you understand why people are willing to leave banks in favor of seemingly riskier investments. You now also understand why financial advisors like me discourage people from leaving banks unless they plan to keep their money invested for at least seven to ten years, and preferably longer. And, finally, you

---

[23] Order now! Operators are standing by!

understand why advisors, like me, encourage our clients to invest in a wide variety of asset classes, and to select a large number of investments within each of those classes.

In other words, instead of trying to pick hot stocks, successful investors focus their energy on the *asset allocation* decision. They begin by asking themselves one question: What asset classes do I want to own?

There's a lot to choose from, including:

Cash Equivalents

Bonds

Stocks

Real Estate

International Securities

Precious Metals

Natural Resources

Commodities

Collectibles

After you slice your pie among these nine major asset classes, you must then determine which sectors to buy within each asset class. To wit:

Cash Equivalents
    Savings Accounts
    Checking Accounts
    Money Markets
    Certificates of Deposit
    U.S. Treasury Bills and EE Savings Bonds
Bonds
    U.S. Government and Agency Securities
    Municipal Bonds
    High Quality Corporate Bonds
    High-Yield (junk) Bonds

Stocks
    Large Cap vs. Small Cap
    Growth vs. Value
    Specific Industry Sectors (such as technology, financial services, manufacturing, cyclicals, automotive, retailing, airlines, pharmaceuticals, and more)
Real Estate
    Residential
    Commercial
    Speculative (raw land)
International Securities
    Stocks vs. Bonds
    Global vs. Continental vs. Nation-Specific
Precious Metals
    Gold
    Silver
    Platinum
Natural Resources
    Minerals
    Oil & Gas
    Lumber and Paper
Commodities
    Options
    Futures
Collectibles
    Stamps
    Coins
    Gemstones
    Artwork
    Sports Memorabilia
    Other Collectibles

Only when you determine which sectors you want to own are you ready to choose specific holdings. And this is where it gets dicey: If you think it's hard enough to determine, say, that 25% is the proper allocation for small cap growth stocks,[24] think again, because the *real* work is still ahead of you: you now must actually select the stocks that will constitute this portion of your portfolio.

Rather than suffering through this decision, a great many investors today simply choose mutual funds. With 10,000 funds in the marketplace, you can find funds to handle virtually any allocation model you might create—including those that specialize in small cap growth stocks.

Will mutual funds make as much money as the top stocks? Of course not. By definition, they can't—for the simple reason that each mutual fund owns dozens, even hundreds, of stocks. And this extensive diversification effectively prevents mutual funds from earning as much money as one given stock might earn. But, of course, this very trait also insures that no mutual fund will ever lose as much as the worst stocks, either. So although you might not earn the most, you won't lose the most, either. But what is far more likely is that mutual funds will produce a much higher profit for you over time than you're likely to obtain by investing in individual stocks and bonds on your own.[25]

After you buy your investments—whether individual securities or mutual funds—you have just one thing more to do: stay invested for a long time. Otherwise, you just might have been better off in those CDs.

---

[24] Hypothetical! Just for instance! Not for real! Not suggested, intended or implied that you really should do this! Example! Example! Example!

[25] If you don't agree with this statement, buy your own stocks and bonds. If you do agree, choose mutual funds. If you're not sure, choose mutual funds—because if you try to find out whether you agree or disagree by picking your own investments, you'll cost yourself a fortune. As my father told me while teaching me to drive: If you know you can cross the intersection safely, do it. If you know you can't, don't try. And if you're not sure, don't try until you *are* sure. My dad's advice has saved my butt more than once.

Misusing The Force

Pretty convincing stuff, this diversification thing. So much so that stockbrokers now call themselves "financial consultants" to distance themselves from the commonly-held (and often legitimate) perception that all they do is buy and sell stocks for their clients. No, not today's brokers: they want to talk to you about your asset allocation model![26]

Unfortunately, a little information can go a long way—a long way, that is, to insuring your poverty. This is because most of the people who preach diversification and asset allocation fail to explain that this strategy is intended only for use under very specific circumstances, and if your circumstances do not match these criteria, then the application of this strategy could be quite detrimental to you, rather than beneficial.

Let me explain.

Diversification is based on mathematical formulations. It assumes two fundamental facts: that you have a pool of assets to invest *right now*, and that you plan to keep those assets invested for a certain amount of time. Many people, however, diversify their assets without meeting both of these conditions—with often disastrous results. Imagine that your doctor has prescribed medication for you, which needs to be taken every four hours for 10 days. You decide, because you're feeling fine after taking just one pill, that you'll not bother with the rest. Or perhaps you'll decide to take them all at once![27] Clearly, a good strategy improperly implemented will lead to poor results.

And so it is with diversification. It can be downright harmful if you apply the strategy improperly. And that's exactly what millions of investors are doing. Want proof? Look no further than your company retirement plan.

---

[26] Which is fine with me, provided they know what they're talking about.

[27] My family regularly fights over this issue. If two aspirins get rid of your headache in 20 minutes, will four aspirins get rid of it in 10 minutes?

These days, most employers who offer a retirement plan let the employees decide for themselves how they want their money invested. To accommodate each employee's preferences, most plans offer a variety of investment options, usually at least four or five (and often 10–20 or more) including:

- a fixed account, which offers a fixed, CD-like return

- a bond mutual fund, which invests in government securities and corporate bonds

- a blue-chip stock fund, which invests in large, well-known companies

- an aggressive growth stock fund, which invests in the stocks of smaller companies

- shares of the employer's stock, if the company is publicly traded

Each worker is free to put all of his or her contributions into just one choice, or split the money among as many or as few of the choices as he or she likes, in any combination.

Who Controls The Force?

Employee control over their allocation decision is a recent development in the world of retirement planning, but the change wasn't made in the name of employee empowerment. Rather, it came about for the benefit of the boss. In other words, nobody suggested that employees would make more money by managing their own assets; instead, the boss merely wanted to avoid the threat of a lawsuit. Why might the boss get sued? Because the employees might be unhappy with the boss's investment results.

You see, retirement plan assets were traditionally managed by employers on behalf of their employees. Not only did employees not have control over how their money was being invested, they often didn't even know how the money was being invested.

As you might imagine, a few employers did a frightfully poor job at managing the money entrusted to them by their employees. In some cases where employers managed to lose money in the plan, instead of growing it, disgruntled employees sued, and the courts often agreed that employers who invested poorly were liable for the losses they incurred. Result: the boss had to reimburse the employees' accounts.

Now, suppose you're an employer, and you manage your company's retirement plan assets. Your goal is to invest the money on behalf of your staff. But your lawyer informs you that if the investments lose money, you could be held personally liable for the losses. What will you do?

That's easy: if you can be held responsible for losses, you'll just make sure there aren't any! And the easiest way to do that is to move all the plan's assets to bank CDs. Your employees might not be earning as much as they could elsewhere, but you've greatly reduced (if not eliminated) your risk of losing money. And with the reduced risk of investment loss, you've reduced the risk of being sued.

One employer in the upper Northwest did exactly this. Through much of the 1980s, he placed 100% of his company's retirement plan assets into bank CDs. Thus, through the entire bull market of the '80s, his employees watched their accounts grow at the rate of about 6% per year.

During this time, however, the stock market gained 15% per year. The employees sued. This time, the boss was not held liable for losses, because there weren't any. Instead, the company was held liable for the *lost profits*. Indeed, the court held that if the employer had managed the money more prudently, the retirement plan would have earned more than 6%. Therefore, the court ruled, the boss had to pay his staff the money they failed to earn as a result of the plan being placed into investments that didn't earn enough.

So what's an employer to do? If the investments you choose lose money, you're liable. If the investments you choose make some money—but not enough—you're liable again. What's an employer to do?

Simple: quit managing your employees' money. Instead, let each staffer choose his or her own investments. Just give them a variety of choices, sufficient to enable them to invest in anything they might want. Then provide them with information about those choices. And finally, get out of their way. Result: the boss's liability is virtually eliminated, because the boss is no longer involved in the investment decision.

There's only one problem: the employees—many of whom have never invested before and who don't know the first thing about it—are now solely responsible for managing their own retirement assets. If they make the right decisions, they'll enjoy a comfortable retirement. But if they make the wrong decision . . .

So here you are. You're in a mandatory meeting about your company retirement plan. Your fellow workers surround you. In the front is some Wall Street type talking about the plan. He's using words like "pre-tax contributions" and "compliance testing." You look around. Some of the staff aren't listening. Others are confused. A few are studying the handouts. The speaker concludes, and asks for questions.

"Do we have to make our own choices?" one asks. Yes, the speaker replies.

"Which choice is the best one?" another says. That's for each person to decide, the speaker replies.

"Which one of these can't lose money?" a third wants to know. The fixed account, the speaker answers. But you shouldn't focus merely on the possibility of losing money, he adds.

"Easy for you to say," a fourth staffer mumbles. "You haven't got child support to pay."

When the meeting is done and the sheets containing each person's selections are turned in, the results are clear: more than 40% of the workers have selected the fixed account for all of their contributions. They've decided to let 100% of their money reside in an account that is likely to pay about 5% per year.[28]

Fortunately, you know a lot more about investing than the average worker. You own investments, and you've done a fair amount of reading on the subject. And you know about the concept of diversification. Consequently, you make a much more prudent decision with your retirement plan allocation form: you split the money among many of the choices, creating a diversified portfolio—just as you do with the rest of your assets. You even try to mentor some of the other staff, to show them the error of their ways, and hoping they'll change their allocation decision. Some listen, some don't.[29]

But as you sit there,[30] thankful that you are more knowledgeable about investment management and comfortable that you've made the right allocation decision, there's something you need to know.

The most successful investors in America don't diversify the money they have in their company retirement plans. Indeed, 50% of our survey respondents are still working full-time, and of this group:

- 96% participate in their company retirement plan. Their average contribution is 10% of pay

- 84% of those participating contribute the maximum

---

[28] I'm not joking here. Although my story is fictitious, the statistics are real: 42% of all 401(k) assets in the U.S. are invested in fixed accounts. It's the most popular choice of American workers. It's also—as you well know—the worst choice.

[29] The story is still fictitious, but the statistics are still real. Asked where they get advice on investing their retirement plan assets, employee surveys show that the number one source is . . . *other employees* (24%). In fact, more workers get advice from *no one* (13%) than from financial advisors (9%). Now, really.

[30] Which you're doing, unless you're reading this book standing up, which is unlikely. Unless you're in a bookstore, in which case you need to close the book and take it to the register already. Now. Really.

And where are they investing the money they contribute to their company retirement plan? According to our survey:

- 87% contribute nothing to bond funds
- 75% contribute nothing to fixed accounts
- 73% contribute nothing to balanced funds
- 90% contribute nothing to employer stock

Where, then, are they placing all their money? For the most part, into some combination of U.S. and international stocks.

What do they know that you don't?

To understand, let's return to the allocation decision you faced in that meeting. As you know, you could have placed all of your money into the fixed account. Ugh. Let's not go there (having already done so in this book.)

You also could have placed 20% in each of the five choices (or in some other combination) so that you are highly diversified. But you know that's wrong. (Though I haven't explained why yet. Hang in there; we'll get to it.)

This leaves you with just one choice left: to invest 100% of your contributions into stocks.

But, my goodness, that certainly isn't a very comfortable way to invest, is it? After all, what if the stock market crashes? All your money would be gone!! Right?

Wrong.[31]

When I wanted you to understand the concept of diversification, we first had to explore the notion of investment selection. We have a similar situation at this point. In order for you to understand why diversification is an incorrect strategy for determining your retirement plan's allocation, we must first explore how that plan works—so you can see if the two are compatible. And, as you'll discover, they aren't.

---

[31] And it wasn't even a nice try.

To begin, ask yourself the one simple question that all investors ask: when is the best time to invest?

This is not a trick question, nor is it academic. And when you ask a roomful of people, you get lots of answers. Some people say the best time to invest is when prices are low. Others say the best time is when you plan to leave the money invested for a long time.

And the most common response: <u>NOW</u>!

But <u>NOW</u>! is not necessarily true. For one thing, it assumes you have money to invest, which you may not. Also, by ignoring whether prices are low, this answer fails to deal with the critical issue of *where* to invest.

But the <u>NOW</u>! advocates do make one very important point: by failing to invest <u>NOW</u>! (often due to procrastination) you fail to earn the profits that could have been made <u>NOW</u>! For this reason, the <u>NOW</u>! advocates are not wrong. Just incomplete.

These answers aren't bad, but they aren't enough, either. So, here's my contribution to the answer: The best time to invest is *when you have the money*. After all, if you don't have any money, it's a pretty lousy time to invest, eh?

So let's put all three components into the formula: the best time to invest is when...

- you have money to invest,

- you plan to invest that money for a long time, and

- prices are low.

Sounds too simple, doesn't it? It's so obvious, anyone would know this, huh? Well, then, how come you didn't articulate this answer a moment ago?[32]

---

[32] For the simple reason that, sometimes, the most obvious answers elude us.

Let's see how (and whether) we can properly apply this principle when investing. Say you have $100,000 in a bank account.[33] To satisfy the advocates, we're going to do this NOW! So, ask yourself The Three Questions:

1) Do you have money to invest? *Obviously*! you say.

2) Do you plan to invest your money for a long time? (*Sure!*, or at least, we'll assume so for this example).

3) Are prices low? *Um*

I said, are prices low? *uhhh*

Uh oh.

Houston, we have a problem.

We don't know if prices are low. And therefore, we don't know if NOW! is truly the best time to invest. And this uncertainty is why we keep our money in the bank and out of the market.[34]

This kind of thinking will keep you out of the market forever. Because you'll never know whether today's prices are low relative to future prices. But this is not the problem you think it is.

In fact, it's the *answer* to our investment management problems.

Here's why. We know we want to invest when prices are low. But we don't know if current prices meet that criterion. And this is where many investors fail. They regard the situation in absolute terms: you either are in or out—your money either is in banks or in stocks.

But this is incorrect. In truth, you're not supposed to be choosing between bank accounts and stocks. Instead, the

---

[33] We'll ignore where it came from. But your spouse might want to know.

[34] 'Tis true. There's more than $1.5 trillion in bank passbook savings accounts in the U.S.—earning the whopping rate of 2% per year.

proper question is whether you want your money to be in bank accounts or stocks—or bonds, or real estate, or gold, or internationals, or natural resources, or, or, or.

In other words, our uncertainty doesn't keep us out of stocks. It merely keeps us from putting *all our money* into stocks. Thus, it's not a question of *when* to invest (because we know the correct answer is <u>NOW</u>!) but rather, *where* to invest. Foolish investors try to determine when to leave the bank, while informed investors know they're leaving—and thus, they focus instead on where to put their money after they've left.

Does the word *diversification* come to mind?

So, in the end, we fully understand why diversification has its place in the investing world. It is ideally suited for those occasions when you have money to invest and you plan to leave that money invested for a long time. Through diversification, you can confidently invest <u>NOW</u>! without worrying whether prices are low—because some prices will be, while others will not. Ultimately, thanks to diversification, your average return will be just fine.

With this information tucked away, let's see if we can repeat the process with your retirement plan assets. To keep this example as simple as possible, let's pretend that you've just joined the company, and you're filling out the papers to enroll in the retirement plan. You've already checked the box indicating you want to contribute the maximum permitted (the equivalent of investing <u>NOW</u>!), which, as you've seen, 84% of my clients are doing.

So let's proceed with The Three Questions:

1) Do you have money to invest in the plan?

I said, do you have money to invest in the plan?

Oh, great. We're off to a fine start. Hey, why are you hesitating? Because, even though the question is simple enough, the answer isn't. *Yes*, you're thinking, *I do have money to invest in the plan. But not right now. I mean, I soon will have money to invest in the plan. But I have to wait until I get my paycheck, because that's where the money I'm putting into the plan is coming from. So, yes, I do have money to invest in the plan, just not right now.*

I'll take a "no" on that, then: you do not have money to invest right now. Before you try to object, let's move on to the next question.

2) Once you get the money, do you plan to invest it for a long time? *Well, yes, of course. Sure. But . . .*

But what?

Well, I won't be getting all the money all at once. Instead, I'll be getting some of it from the next paycheck, and some more of it from the paycheck after that, and so on. As a result, I'll have some money to invest next week—and that money certainly will be invested for a long time—but other money I invest will be from future paychecks, and I won't be getting some of that money for many years to come. Thus, some of the money I contribute won't be invested for as long a period as some of my earlier contributions.

Okay, I'll give you a "maybe" or "sometimes" on that one. Let's move on.

3) Are prices low? *What do you mean?*

What do you mean, "What do I mean?" <u>Are prices low</u>?

Well, today, they might be low, or they might be high. I don't know. But since I'm investing money with each paycheck, prices are certain to be different each time. So even if I try to answer your question for today's paycheck, the answer for the next paycheck will be different. It's impossible to give an effective answer.

Okay, let's see what we've got here. The last time we asked ourselves The Three Questions, we obtained clear, simple answers. And those answers showed us that diversification was the proper strategy. But this time, we're floundering. We don't have the money right now, but we'll soon get some. And we won't get it all—at least, not all at once. Instead, we'll get it slowly over a very long period of time. And during this time, prices will vary dramatically.

Thus, the answers do not point to diversification this time. Diversification, as we've learned, is designed for the management of assets you already have. But we have no assets. Instead, we simply know that we're going to get some assets in the future. Diversification also demands that our money be invested for long periods. And although most of the money we'll be investing will remain so for long periods, some of it will not be. Thus, diversification is not the ideal investment strategy for our retirement plan assets.

What, then, is?

The answer is right in front of us. If the strengths of diversification are weaknesses when it comes to our retirement plan, then we should be able to convert the weaknesses of diversification into strengths for our retirement plan.

So let's examine the situation. The plan's investments don't change. The frequency of our paychecks doesn't change. And the amount of money we contribute from each paycheck doesn't change. But the prices do change—constantly. So let's see if we can exploit these facts to our advantage.

We know each investment has a different price. We also know that, for some investments, prices fluctuate a lot, while for other investments, they never fluctuate. In the fixed account, for example, values never change (which is why you don't lose money in those accounts), while stock prices change daily.

So, to determine which is the best way to invest, let's examine the results of two hypothetical strategies. In the first, we'll put all of our contributions into the fixed account, where prices never change. In the second, we'll choose stocks, where prices change a lot. For this exercise, we'll assume you are paid monthly, and that you contribute $100 to your plan with each paycheck.

Let's look first at the results from investing in the fixed account. In Month One, we add $100. The principal value never fluctuates, so the $100 is always worth $100. But the account earns interest, at the rate of 6% per year.[35] Therefore, at the end of Year One, this $100 contribution will be worth $106. In Month Two, you'll add another $100. It too will grow at the rate of 6%, but because it's invested for only 11 months, it's worth just $105.50 after one year. Thus, each month's contribution grows a little bit less than the contribution made before it, because each is invested for less time than the prior contributions. If you repeat this process for 12 months, you'll discover that the ending value of your account is $1,239, of which $1,200 was your own capital. That means the profit was $35.

Now, let's compare this to the stock fund. We start by adding $100 to the stock fund in Month One. We'll pretend that the price per share is $10. Now, Month Two comes along, and we add another $100 to the account. But what is the price of the fund now? We can't assume it's still $10 per share like last month, because stock prices fluctuate.

So we need to make certain assumptions about what the next stock price is going to be. And it's obvious that our guess will have a big impact on the results. So, let's run four separate tests. In the first test, we'll have the share price drop every month. In the second, we'll increase it every month. In the third, we'll lower the price for several months but then increase it in the later months, so that the price at the end of the year is the same as where it started (meaning the fund itself enjoys no net gain or loss). And in the fourth, we'll do the opposite: we'll initially increase the price but later decrease it, again ending where we started (and again, with no net gain or loss in the fund).

---

[35] This rate varies from plan to plan, and from year to year, but 6% is a reasonable estimate for our purposes. And to make our lives (okay, my life) simpler, we're using simple interest.

Thus, the monthly prices for our four experiments look like this:

Month	Falling Market	Rise-Then-Fall Market	Fall-Then-Rise Market	Rising Market
1	$10	$10	$10	$10
2	$9	$11	$9	$11
3	$8	$12	$8	$12
4	$7½	$13	$7	$13
5	$7	$14	$6	$14
6	$6	$15	$5	$15
7	$5½	$15	$5	$16
8	$5	$14	$6	$17
9	$4	$13	$7	$18
10	$3	$12	$8	$19
11	$2	$11	$9	$20
12	$1	$10	$10	$21

And here are the values of each fund after investing $100 per month for one year:

The Falling Market Fund:	$ 324
The Rising–Falling Fund:	$ 979
The Falling–Rising Fund:	$1,691
The Rising Market Fund:	$1,714

Let's see if we can draw any conclusions from this data. The results from both the Falling Market Fund and the Rising Market Fund are pretty much what you'd expect: when stocks steadily fall, you lose money, and when they steadily rise, you make money. No surprises there.

It's also not terribly helpful, because the stock market never acts either way; it doesn't go down and stay down, nor does it go up and stay up. Instead, the market jumps around a lot— gaining or losing one time, and losing or gaining at other times. So let's dismiss these two choices as simply unrealistic.

Therefore, let's focus our attention on the other two funds. And the message they offer is clear: the Falling-Rising Fund made more money ($1,691) than the Rising-Falling Fund ($979).

This is an incredibly important discovery, because it directly counters the very argument that people offer for not wanting to invest in stocks. *I am afraid to put my retirement plan contributions into stock funds because the price might go down.* Good! As the Falling-Rising Fund shows, this is exactly why you should invest there.

In other words, instead of being concerned that your retirement plan contributions might fall in value, you should be thrilled—because experiencing lower values with early contributions will enable you to enjoy higher gains in the future. I know this sounds counterintuitive (like I warned you in the introduction, remember) but that's how money really works.

To prove this point, let's return to the Falling Markets Fund. Sure, it's worth only $324 after one year (after investing $1,200), but is it really such a loser?

Not at all. To understand why, let's review its performance:

Month	Amount Invested	Share Price
1	$100	$10
2	$100	$9
3	$100	$8
4	$100	$7½
5	$100	$7
6	$100	$6
7	$100	$5½
8	$100	$5
9	$100	$4
10	$100	$3
11	$100	$2
12	$100	$1

Based on this information, I ask you: To what level must the share price rise in order for you to break even?

If you think you'd need to return to the mid-point, $5.67 per share, you're wrong. The mid-point is the average price you paid over the full 12 months. But you don't need the stock fund to return to that level. Instead, it merely needs to grow to $3.70 in order for you to break even. If the price were indeed to grow to $5.67, your account would be worth $1,839.42—giving you a $639 profit!

Even more remarkably, if the price were to return to its original $10 level, your account would be worth an astonishing $3,244!

If you're like most readers, you find this quite surprising. That's because you don't normally invest small amounts of money at regular intervals over long periods. Instead, you typically invest only occasionally, and when you do, you deal with relatively large amounts of money.

Because retirement plan participants invest in an unusual way, the mathematical results are themselves unusual. To understand why, let me share with you one figure I've omitted throughout our discussion.

So far, we've considered the *amount invested* and the *price per share*. What we have not yet examined is the *number of shares obtained*. And this, as you'll see, is why our example needs to earn only $3.70 to reach the break-even point.

Consider the following:

Month	Amount Invested	Share Price	Number of Shares Obtained
1	$100	$10	10.000
2	$100	$9	11.111
3	$100	$8	12.500
4	$100	$7½	13.333
5	$100	$7	14.286
6	$100	$6	16.667
7	$100	$5½	18.182
8	$100	$5	20.000
9	$100	$4	25.000
10	$100	$3	33.333
11	$100	$2	50.000
12	$100	$1	100.000
	$1,200	$68	324.412

Study carefully the relationship between the last two columns. As you can see, as the price falls, you buy an increasing number of shares. This is why the average price per share is $3.70, not $5.67. You see, $3.70 is derived as follows:

$$\frac{\text{total amount invested}}{\text{total number of shares}} = \frac{\$1,200}{324.412} = \$3.70$$

While $5.67 is obtained this way:

$$\frac{\text{average price per share}}{\text{total number of months}} = \frac{\$68}{12} = \$5.67$$

Do you see the difference between the two equations? The first deals with the number of shares you own and the money you invested, while the second focuses on the average prices you paid and the number of months it took you to acquire them.

Both answers are correct, of course. But they are giving you different pieces of information. What you learn from the second equation is that $5.67 is the *average price* that your shares are worth, while the first equation is the *average cost* of those shares.

Now, look again:

The average price is $5.67
The average cost is $3.70

If this investment method has you forever paying the *average cost* for shares that are forever worth a higher *average price*, doesn't it seem to suggest that this method produces for you a built-in profit? Absolutely!

This method, to finally get around to naming it, is called dollar cost averaging. Like diversification, it works very well— but only under certain conditions. They are as follows:

1) you must invest a specific amount of money,

2) you must invest this money at a regular interval,

3) the money you are investing must be money you have only recently obtained, and

4) you must maintain this system for long periods of time.

Without question, your retirement plan is the ideal vehicle to take advantage of dollar cost averaging, because your paycheck is the same each pay period and the amount you place into your plan is the same each time, too. And because you get paid at regular intervals, your contributions are made at regular intervals as well. Third, the reason you are waiting to invest the money today is that you were only paid today; you didn't invest this money last week simply because you didn't have the money last week. And finally, you're going to be working for a very long time—for years and probably even for decades. That's more than enough time for dollar cost averaging to ride the waves of the market's volatile performance.

Thanks to dollar cost averaging, you don't have to worry whether the market is up or down. When the price is high (relative to other times), you simply will not purchase many shares (relative to other purchases). But when the price is low, the system will automatically obtain for you a higher number of shares. Therefore, dollar cost averaging is certain to produce for you the lowest average cost, and that puts you in a great position to enjoy profits.

This is why my firm's clients place so much of their retirement plan contributions into stocks.

If you're still not convinced, consider this: In most plans, your employer puts money into the plan for you, called a "basic contribution." Many employers also match your contributions, sometimes even dollar-for-dollar. If your employer does this, you've doubled your money before it gets invested! In other words, if you put in a dollar and your boss puts in a dollar, you've got two dollars. Thus, even if your account falls by 50%, your dollar remains intact. So don't fret that choosing 100% stocks will place your money at risk, for you're really just placing *your boss's money at risk.*

And even a total loss isn't as bad as it sounds. Say you've been in the plan for 15 years and suddenly, the stock fund drops in value to zero. A crisis? Not at all, and here's why: If you're 50 years old and planning to work until age 65, you've got 360 paychecks yet to come—and all of those future contributions to your retirement plan will be at the stock fund's new low price! When stocks finally recover over the next 15 years, you'll make a fortune! Indeed, a stock market crash would be the best thing that could happen to you!

A few more points on dollar cost averaging before we're finished.

Through all of this analysis, we've completely ignored two other considerations. First, we ignored the alternative of selecting the fixed account for our contributions. And second, we ignored the idea of putting all our money into company stock, instead of stock mutual funds. Let's look at these issues. First, the fixed account.

Clearly, the fixed account made more money ($1,239) than our Rising-Falling Fund ($979). But this example covered only the first 12 months of the total career performance. What do you suppose will be the situation after two years? After 20 years?

You see, after two years, the fixed account will continue to plod along, earning 6% per year. Thus, after you'd invested $2,400 over 24 months, your account will be worth $2,550 (thanks to compounding). And the Rising-Falling Fund? Well, if Year Two performs identically to Year One, it'll be worth just $1,958—twice as much after Year Two as it was after Year One. But do you really think the stock price will end each year precisely where it began, year after year and decade after decade? Highly improbable. Indeed, the example itself suggests otherwise, because we increased the share price to $15 during the year before returning it to $10. And at $15, that fund after two years is worth $2,936—substantially more than the fixed account.

History proves this point. Since 1970, the average annual bank CD rate has been 7.15%. If you invested $100 per year at that rate through December 1998, you'd have contributed a total of $2,900, and your account would be worth $8,964. However, if you instead invested that annual contribution of $100 into the stock market, your account value as of December 31, 1998, would have been $20,296.

And what about buying company stock with your retirement plan contributions?

Don't do it—regardless of how successful your company is or how successful you expect it to be.

The reason: buying company stocks is highly speculative. You see, it's one thing if a stock you own falls in value. This might (and indeed, will) happen to one (or some) of the many stocks you own inside a mutual fund. But if you own only one stock, and if that one stock plummets in value, the results could be devastating to you.

Even more so if that stock happens to be of the company you work for. A crashing stock price means the company is in financial trouble. Under those circumstances, the company may take radical steps to save money. Quickest way: cut the staff. In other words, a declining price in your company stock could cause you to lose your job. And if that happened, you'd need to start selling investments to help you pay your bills. But you could find that the biggest investment you own is—guess what?—company stock!

Thus, just as you need the cash, you discover that it's value has been sliced by Wall Street. And the reason you need to sell it is the very reason you can't sell it for much. That's quite a predicament to be in—and one you should avoid.

Unfortunately, few workers are aware of this advice. Among 401(k) plans that offer employer stock as an investment option, 42% of all assets are placed there. I don't know if the reason is misguided loyalty, unrealistic expectations regarding future value, or the Proud Parent effect (it's my company, so it's clearly the best!), but it's dangerous. Consider: 92% of the money in Coca-Cola's 401(k) plan is invested in Coca-Cola stock. *Ninety-two percent.* It's a great deal for Coke—the company gets to match contributions with stock instead of cash (that's much cheaper for the company), but it's downright foolish for the employees.

Some will disagree with this. Coke, for example, is a fabulous company, they'll argue. It'll always do great. To which I say, Oh really? Pilots working for Eastern Airlines once felt the same way. So did IBM employees who retired in the early 1990s. After 30 or 40 years of service, with their retirement plans holding nothing but IBM stock, IBMers watched in horror as IBM's stock price plummeted from $187 a share in August 1993 to $44 just 72 months later. My colleagues and I counseled hundreds of these former employees during that turmoil, and I can assure you: the word "devastating" is not too strong.[36]

Sure, IBM has since recovered from its lows. Which is fine for those who are still with the company and who are still

---

[36] Neither is the word "furious," because these workers felt betrayed by their employer.

contributing to their retirement plan. But for those who were unfortunate enough to be leaving the company just as the market bottomed out? Nearly a lifetime of savings was swept away.

Don't put yourself in this position. If you want to buy company stock, fine. But keep your holdings to less than 15% of your total personal net worth. If you think that doesn't sound like much, consider that professional money managers typically restrict themselves to placing just 5% of assets into any single investment. By this standard, 15% is huge—yet I routinely meet people who have 60%, 70%, or even 90% of their assets tied up in just one stock.

This is foolish. It's also a great concern to financial advisors. A 1999 survey of financial planners, conducted by the International Association for Financial Planning, revealed that:

- 66% of planners said most people do not understand the risks involved with employer stock ownership plans;

- More than half agreed that the biggest mistake employees make is holding employer stock rather than a diversified basket of stocks; and

- Less than 20% of planners surveyed believe that employees understand important employer stock ownership issues, such as insider trading issues and the need to maintain a diversified portfolio.

Believe me, "because I work there" is a dumb reason to be so heavily weighted in one security.

So now you know that the best way to invest your company retirement plan is to place 100% of your contributions entirely into stock mutual funds. Do not diversify, and do not buy company stock (or at least, not much of it). As our survey results show, this is how successful people do it.

But as you implement this strategy, keep three points in mind:

First, stick with it. If you follow the daily (or even monthly) performance of your stock funds, you'll notice them doing poorly from time to time. And during such periods, you'll be tempted to transfer your money out of stocks and into the fixed account, or some other option that's doing better. Resist this temptation. Remember that dollar cost averaging works best with volatile investments, and it's when prices are down that you're really planting the seeds for future profits.

Second, remember that dollar cost averaging requires you to have a long-term investment horizon. Therefore, this strategy is not ideal if you plan to withdraw the money from your retirement account within two or three years—because the stock market might not recover from a crash in such a short period of time. Diversifying would the better choice for people in this situation.

And third, the same rule applies for people who already have a large balance in their retirement accounts. This entire discussion has focused on the money you're adding to your plan with each new paycheck; I have not been referring to the assets already accumulated in the plan itself. If you've already got an account balance of five or six figures, transferring that entire balance to stock funds today is not dollar cost averaging—that's lump sum investing.

These second and third points largely explain why, of the clients who responded to my survey:

- 13% have some assets in bond funds

- 25% have some assets in fixed accounts, and

- 27% have assets in balanced funds

All of the respondents have a substantial amount of money in their company retirement plan, and with 40% of them over the age of 60, it is entirely appropriate for this subset of clients to have a retirement plan that is diversified by many asset classes. But even for this group, stocks continue to dominate their portfolios.

Therefore, when handling your company retirement plan, you should diversify your existing balances and dollar cost average your future contributions. As my clients have shown, that's the best way to create wealth.

SUCCESSFUL INVESTORS:
THEY DON'T DIVERSIFY THE MONEY THEY CONTRIBUTE TO THEIR EMPLOYER RETIREMENT PLANS.
INSTEAD, THEY PUT ALL THEIR CONTRIBUTIONS INTO ONE ASSET CLASS—THE ONE FEW OTHERS CHOOSE.
"IN THEIR OWN WORDS"

I've been putting money into my company plan for years. All the money is going into stocks—25% international, 25% small company, 25% big company, and 25% in my employer's stock. I earn $100,000+ a year, so participating in the plan is easy. I think it's crazy if you don't participate. In my first two years of working, I didn't participate for some reason, and when I look back now, it was stupid not to contribute. I gave away free money!

I have never borrowed or withdrawn the money from my retirement plan, nor was I ever tempted to do so. I never want to touch that money. Too many other workers fail to contribute the maximum amount. They contribute only the amount that our employer matches. But that's nowhere near as much as you're allowed to contribute. That's a big mistake.

I should have gone to see a planner earlier. I should have done something in my 30s (I started in my 40s). If I did, I would have more money to show for it today. If you start earlier, you have more time to save, and you could retire earlier.

Fred D., project executive. Raised in San Mateo, California

Shelley D., self-employed project manager. Raised in Hillsdale, New Jersey

I started putting money into my company plan when I was 26 years old. I was earning at the time about $32,000, and participating in the plan was easily affordable. The money came directly out of my paycheck. I put the money 100% into stock funds because I felt that offered better returns. Most other employees listened to each other for ideas on where to invest the money. Their biggest mistake was that they didn't contribute the maximum amount. They would only contribute a couple percent of their pay.

Name withheld, software engineer. Raised in Woodbridge, Virginia

---

I was 46 and making $66,000 when I started with my company plan. I felt it was easily affordable, because it was coming directly out of my paycheck; so I never saw the money in the first place.

I've been tempted to move the money out of stocks and into something else at times, but I realize that the market is for long-term investing, and that's what I was doing. You hear and read things, but I will stick with what I'm doing and not change anything.

Name withheld, project manager. Raised in Allen Park, Michigan

Spouse, teacher

I have very little in international stocks (about 10%), and the rest is in large company stocks. I put the 401(k) money in stock mutual funds. I started putting money into the 401(k) when I was 53 years old. I started late. I've learned that it's ridiculous if you don't participate. I used to tell employees to put as much as they can in the plan or they won't be able to afford to retire. Most employees are putting money in the plan, but I don't think they put it in the right places. I think some could put more in, but they don't take it very seriously. They spend too much money on things like snacks and soda. And they go out to lunch all the time instead of bringing it in from home. They should be saving that money instead of spending it. And they do this every day!

Friedel Groene, vice president in charge of electronic hardware manufacturing. Raised in Germany

---

I am an attorney with the federal government. I'm putting all my current contributions into stocks, simply for the fact that I am investing for long-term growth, not short term.

I was 42 years old when I started, earning about $44,000. It wasn't a stretch because I have always done something to save. You have to make the decision to pay yourself first. When I was 21, I told myself to give away 10%, save 10%, and use the rest for bills, and I've stuck to that. My family and I have always had money for ourselves.

You don't miss the money you put into the plan because you don't realize you have it. It comes off the top of the paycheck; just like taxes. It's an easy way to invest.

I tend to pay more attention to finances than most other people. Most people are still going from paycheck to paycheck. You can go from paycheck to paycheck, but you still can save. Some people tell me that they're not putting any money in at all because they can't afford to. My response is, you can't afford not to.

Name withheld, attorney. Raised in Westchester County, New York

Spouse, school librarian

I joined my plan as soon as it was available, and placed all my money into a stock mutual fund. I was 55 years old at the time, earning about $70,000 per year. I didn't feel it was a burden. The plan was there and it was easy. I think people need to seek professional advice on how to select investments. They should get more information on what to select. People are afraid to go into something they perceive as risky.

Name withheld, software project manager for FDIC. Raised in Batesville, Mississippi

———————————— §§ ————————————

I look at my plan as a long-term investment. Time horizon is way out there. Best returns historically have been from stocks, and I figure it will continue that way. I started putting money in the plan when I was 34 years old. I was earning about $50,000 a year at the time.

In 1986, the market had a downturn and I was stupid so I took the money out. I learned my lesson though. If we could go backwards in time, I wouldn't have touched the money.

Name withheld, spy for the CIA

———————————— §§ ————————————

I'm the fiduciary for the company's plan so I talk to people about it quite a bit; it's my job. Too many people do not participate in the plan, and we are constantly trying to increase the number of participants. That's the most common mistake: people are not participating. Or, if they are participating, they are not contributing the maximum. And when they do invest, they don't invest in equities. Instead, they choose guaranteed funds and money markets.

Mark Danisewicz, chief Financial Officer of a major corporation. Kinnelon, New Jersey

Karen A. Danisewicz, homemaker. Raised in Springfield, Virginia

I'm a Foreign Service Officer for the State Department. I've been putting money into the government Thrift Savings Plan ever since the government let me. Everything goes into the stock fund. I put in 10% of my pay. I will work for another couple of decades, so I can handle a few years of downturn and still be ahead of the game. It's a bigger gamble not to do it.

I was 24 years old when I started putting money in, and I was making around $17,000 a year. It hurt at first. When I started, I only contributed 5% of my pay. Then two years later, I thought I was being stupid, so I went to 10% and maxed it out. The easy part was, once I got used to the regular paycheck after the deductions, I learned to live with the weekly allotment. But I also racked up some credit card bills. In retrospect, it was probably better that I racked up the bills and contributed money to the plan at the same time, instead of not contributing to the plan at all. When I finally paid off the credit cards, at least I also had money in the plan.

Today, I don't consider participating in the plan to be a burden. In fact, I see it with some glee. I don't make a huge salary, but nonetheless, I've got a lot money in the plan now.

Co-workers talk about the retirement plan all the time. People talk about shifting their money around within the different choices, and fussing over whether or not they are going to beat the next drop or upturn. I just tell them to leave their money alone and let it ride.

I've seen some workers fail to put anything into the plan. And some put money into the fixed account. I use just the stock fund choice. Putting money into a fund that pays only 5% or 6% is a bigger risk than the stock fund choice, because of inflation.

If I could do things over again, I would have contributed the maximum to the plan in those first couple of years. And I wouldn't have racked up those credit card debts. Another thing, I would have started saving outside the plan early on.

Name withheld. Raised in Birmingham, Michigan

It was easy to contribute to the employer-sponsored retirement plan. There was a certain percentage that we were allowed to put in, and that's what I did. It came directly out of my paycheck, so what I didn't see, I didn't miss. I did not feel it was a burden.

Part of my job was to talk with employees about the plan. Some workers didn't contribute, even though they could afford to. In long run, they hurt themselves financially.

Name withheld, personnel director for the U.S. Department of Defense

———————————— *§§* ————————————

I have been contributing to the Thrift Savings Plan for as long as it has been available to me. It was easy to do. Since the money was taken directly out of my paycheck, I never saw it. If you don't see it, you don't miss it. I wish they'd let us contribute more!

I see a lot of other employees enjoying the "present value" of their money, by going to the movies or what have you, rather than saving the money and enjoying it later in life. They live for today and not for tomorrow.

Linda Jackie, computer systems auditor, Department of the Navy. Raised in Falls Church, Virginia

———————————— *§§* ————————————

I started working for the federal government when I was 22 years old. My starting salary was less than $5,000 a year. And I participated in the retirement plan right away. I didn't feel it was a burden. I never saw the money . . . what you don't have, you don't miss.

Looking back, I wouldn't do anything differently.

I would encourage others to do the same thing: Contribute

the most you can. And put it into the stock fund. The younger you are, the more risk you can take.

Kathleen Hoyt, retired, former deputy director for inspections in the U.S. Government. Raised in Columbia, Missouri

I chose stocks for my retirement plan because I felt the need for a better return; I didn't want to put the money in bonds because it wouldn't have been that profitable over long run. I was 55, earning roughly $65,000 a year, when I started putting money into the company plan.

Charles Duttweiler, publisher at a trade association. Raised in Ridgewood, New York

Dolores Duttweiler, homemaker. Raised in Ridgewood, New York

I started participating in the plan at work when I was 30. It's easy. In fact, I wish I could put even more in than they let me!

Rick Rabil, company president. Raised in Virginia

Sue Rabil, housewife. Raised in Virginia

I started putting money into my retirement plan at work when I was 26. Back then, I was earning $14,000. It wasn't a stretch. We were young and new in the workforce. What really got me started was when *USA Today* had a story on what it would take for Baby Boomers to reach retirement—$1.5 million, they said—and I thought, "Oh, my God." It's really scary—with parents living longer, too, who will take care of them? Plus, we have a young disabled child and an older daughter we need to think about. Fortunately, we both come from families who stressed the need for saving. So we don't regard saving money as a burden. And with the company matching our contributions, you'd be an idiot not to participate. It's free money!

I placed all my money into stocks, since I'm adding money slowly, and I've been tempted to move out of stocks when stocks are plunging. But I try to be realistic about it. Most people are not aggressive enough. They want to know their money is safe and will be there and you undermine yourself by doing that.

Helene, director, membership

Ron, supermarket stocker

I don't work now, and I may never go back. Before we got married, we decided that the goal was for me to stay home when we had a child. So we worked very hard to reduce our debt. Now, we're living on one income and we're not going into our savings to do this. We paid off all our debts—the car and student loans—and we're in the process of buying a house. Before we had our baby, we lived off one income to see if we could do it.

We were only 22 when Todd starting saving in his retirement plan at work, and it was a stretch, but it's not any longer. One of the mistakes couples make is to buy a house based on two salaries and when they have kids and one wants to stay home, they can't because of the mortgage. Couples just starting out should try to live on one paycheck.

Helen, wife and mother

Todd, aerospace engineer

We're comfortable with putting all our retirement plan assets into stocks because stocks have performed better than anything else over very long periods. Since we're leaving this money alone for a long period of time, it seems to be the right thing to do. I wasn't always as knowledgeable as I am now, but I am now comfortable with having the money in stocks.

We were just 24 when we were starting. I was earning $18,000. He was making $38,000. We felt we could easily afford it. We figured if we never saw it, we would never miss it.

People at work tend to listen to each other. A lot of them put their money into the fixed account because that's what others say they are doing. I also saw a lot of people borrowing the money they had in their plan. I'd never do that.

Mary Greer, stay-at-home mom, computer programmer. Raised in Fairfax County, Virginia

Steve Greer, systems engineer. Raised in Vienna, Virginia

Stocks offer the best long-term growth potential. So that's the best way to improve my financial situation. I started when I was 28 or so, making about $32,000. At first, I put in just $100 per paycheck. I was younger and didn't understand the importance of retirement and saving. And I didn't understand the plan. Being young, more immediate needs were sometimes more important. But I learned soon enough and decided to put in the max. And it's the smartest thing I've ever done. From 1979 to 1993, my 401(k) grew to $700,000. That's a lot of money.

The most common mistake I see at work is other workers not getting in the plan as soon as they are eligible. And sometimes they don't contribute as much as they can. Our company matches 50 cents on the dollar, so you're crazy not to contribute the maximum.

The best advice I could give is to get in early, contribute the max, don't try to time the market, be a long-term investor, and don't think short-term when you're dealing with retirement. Even if you're near retirement, you should be thinking long term, because you're going to live 20 years or so after retirement! So don't think short term.

Jay, lobbyist

Sharon, art teacher

We both have been putting money into our retirement plans since we were 22. What really got me motivated was a chart I saw showing how much money you'll need to be able to retire. We put it all into stocks because we need all the help we can get!

We regard the plan as a necessity. We live pretty tight, and although our net worth has gone up—we still put everything into the 401(k). You might say that we save more than we earn, instead of spending more than we earn. We have no debts but the mortgage.

It was hard at first to join the retirement plan. We had massive student loans—$700 a month for about five years. We decided to live on her salary and invest mine. It was tough, because we were so consumption-oriented after school. But we did it. I got a Masters and B.S. at Northwestern University in four years—shaving off two years, which saved a lot of money. My wife got her BS in just three years. I was very aware of all the money I was wasting on classes that I didn't want to take but had to for requirements, so to save money, I did internships that gave me full credit.

When I was 21, my boss said I'd be an idiot if I didn't take advantage of the retirement plan. So I've tried to tell others. It often doesn't work. My wife has tried to educate two of her friends. Neither has contributed a dime, but Laura has six figures in her plan. Her co-workers can't believe how much she has and yet they still won't contribute. Instead, all their money goes to clothing and trips.

It's striking how many do not participate. And a lot who do put money in the fund choose the wrong option. They put it into the fixed account, or into company stock. The worst thing is seeing people take their money out to buy a house or something.

Name withheld, 34, screenwriter

Spouse, 33, journalist

Given my time horizon, putting the money into stocks is the most appropriate thing to do. It's easy to contribute, because I never see the money, so I never miss it. I wish I could contribute more. Once I made the initial move into stocks, I have been committed to it. I don't want to touch the money.

I think a lot of the new staff listen to other staffers. They take advice from others, and that's not always good.

Name withheld, procurement executive for the U.S. Department of Transportation

Spouse, federal employee

Participating in the plan was a stretch, but I did it anyway, and as time went on, it got easier. Since the money comes directly out of my paycheck, I don't even know it's gone. I think that's a good investment strategy—when you don't even know that it's gone, you can't spend it.

Name withheld, program manager

Spouse, administrative assistant

The biggest financial thing in my life is my 401(k). It did more for my savings than anything else.

Richard Felix

I was about 25 or 26 years old when my company offered a 401(k) retirement plan. This was when I began saving for retirement. I believe I was earning around $25,000. I have always felt that I could easily contribute to the plan. The money comes directly off the top of my paychecks, so since I never see that money, I never miss it. It is important for me to save through my company's 401(k) plan because this is my only retirement plan.

I was too conservative in the beginning—I put everything into the guaranteed fund instead of the stock fund. The guaranteed rate of 8% seemed good at the time. I think this was from my lack of knowledge of the stock market. By learning about investing and the history of the stock market, I saw how much better my money could do. I have since reallocated my 401(k) contributions.

Jim Mosesso, government contractor. Raised in Pittsburgh, Pennsylvania

Catherine Mosesso, works for the U.S. Government. Raised in Bel Air, Maryland

---

I have been putting money into the company retirement plan since 1972, when I was 23 years old and just out of graduate school. I think I was earning $700 a month. I've long felt that putting the money into stocks would give me the highest rate of return. I made the decision by meeting with planners and reading.

I made a lot of errors in my plan that I would fix if I could. For one thing, I made some withdrawals in the late 1970s to buy a house and other assets, and I wish I hadn't done that, because my 401(k) would be worth a lot more today if I hadn't made that withdrawal. And at other times, I moved out of stocks and into either bonds or guaranteed investments. If we could go backwards in time, I would not have done that, either.

I would have kept the money in equities. And I would not have invested so heavily in the company I work for.

Charlie Shipp, government relations. Raised in Dallas, Texas

I made the decision to put the money in stocks because I just felt stocks was the best bet over the long haul. I looked at the history of long-term investing. I didn't start until I was 40 years old. At the time, I believe I was earning about $34,000. I discovered that it's easy to contribute to the retirement plan. I don't even miss it. The money goes in, and I forget all about it. I don't see the money, so I don't miss it. Really, I don't think about it; it's like it's not even there.

I don't listen to the people at work. I think there is a herd mentality. I've pretty much made up my mind as to what I want to do.

L.A. Quezada, management analyst. Raised in Pittsburg, California

My husband and I started saving for retirement 10 years ago. We put all our contributions into stocks because we planned to leave the money there for the long term, not short term. We were in our mid 40s when we started. I was making $30,000; my husband, $80,000.

I noticed that most of the younger workers weren't getting involved in the plan. It was hard to convince them to. Most other people I saw were putting some money in but not as much as they could. I think I was the only one doing the maximum, and I think I was the only one who chose the stock fund. One co-worker pulled his out of stocks after the Crash of '87 and he never put it back.

If I had to summarize the mistakes I saw others make, I'd say: never getting started. And being too conservative. People should put in all you're allowed and invest more in stocks.

Name withheld, auditor

I started putting money into my employer's retirement plan when I was 38. I was then earning $24,000 a year. It was a stretch at first.

When co-workers talk about the retirement plan, the conversation is typically about the fact that if they had started sooner, they could probably be retired by now and living off the investments. Most workers live for today. They don't understand the necessity of taking care of yourself for the future. They just spend their paychecks and enjoy themselves right now. Some workers put in just the minimum, which is $25 a month. I put in the max. And a lot of people put money in for safety. They don't give themselves the chance to earn higher returns. I've noticed unbelievable earnings with my plan. I would tell people to invest for the long term, not the short term.

John Barrow, public safety employee. Raised in Columbia, Maryland

---

Given that I have such a long time before retirement, contributing 100% to stocks in my plan makes the most sense. I wish I could contribute more, but I'm not allowed to. Because the money comes off the top of your paycheck, you don't have to worry about it. If you do get involved, you need to avoid second-guessing yourself. Stick to your guns and go for the long haul.

Brad Primeau, program manager. Raised in Bay City, Michigan

I felt it was easy to contribute. The money was taken off the top of my paycheck for my 401(k). I have not yet been tempted to move the money around, so it will probably stay in some kind of stock fund.

I see people investing in our company stock, but I think it's a mistake to do that. It's not diversified.

Name withheld, pilot

Spouse, flight attendant

As a student counselor, I was involved in the state retirement program from the very beginning, since 1965. At the start, I was earning $7,500 a year. In 1975 I joined the Supplemental Retirement Program on a voluntary basis. I retired in 1997.

Job security was never great. I went from year to year trying to justify my job at the university. Eventually the president was forced to retire. And in 1990, I got thrown out. But they liked me, so I got a job as Assistant Registrar. Losing my job was the greatest thing that could have happened because it forced me to see I couldn't count on a job for an income. We needed to get the best resources ourselves. I talked to my wife and we decided to get a professional to help us with a financial plan. With the advisor's help, we bought into the philosophy that a long range approach is the only way to invest and that you want a diversified portfolio. We got to where we are now from no management to management.

My grandfather was working after three heart attacks because he couldn't afford to stop. So I learned the lesson from him. That was my motivation to join the retirement plan. We bought a house a year later, in 1972, and we scraped by. I repaired my own car. We did a lot of things to get by. The advice we got from the retirement system reps really made a difference.

I was fortunate to live in New Zealand before I graduated

from college. People there didn't need all the materials things we need here. I learned the value of saving. In the U.S., we have such a regard for consumption, but I felt I didn't need to live that way. My upbringing taught me that saving was important, but I never understood until the mid-70s that there was such a thing as investing. I didn't understand risk.

Sometimes, you're influenced by the people around you. I once met a fellow naval reservist who said he never bought a new car because it's too expensive. That reinforced the idea that you could save. I could drive an old car and let my neighbor buy a new one and other expensive things. I don't need to compete on that level. It's a mind set.

It's important that you be able to think for yourself, and not blindly do what your parents did. My father's attitude was that the stock market was a bad thing. He worked as a courier on Wall Street in 1929 and he saw someone jump during the crash. That type of experience changes you, and all through his life he thought the market was something you didn't get involved with.

But I didn't follow his advice. My parents taught me to save, but I learned to invest. I never had the urge to take the money and run. In 1987, my investments dropped 30%, but I let it ride and I've done well ever since. But others got out.

Despite the uncertainty I faced with my job every year, I never borrowed from my retirement plan. Other workers used to talk about the fact that they didn't have enough money to save, but we were all earning similar amounts of money. My parents had saved and I saw how tough it was on them. I wanted to be financially independent. I realized that you can't let your job be your life. I was always performing "above and beyond" at my job, but I realized that institutions can't protect you. It's up to you to see to it that you're financially independent. Once you're financially independent, you don't have to fear losing your job. It makes you a better staffer—knowing that you're working because you want to, not just because you have to. That's what I try to pass on to my family.

John, retired

I've been investing in the stock fund all my married life. I knew that the safe accounts, earning a 6% rate, would not serve us well. So I put the money into the stock fund.

A lot of people still think investing in stocks is a crap shoot, like going to Vegas. That's too bad.

I wasn't able to start contributing until I was 56. I was then earning $40,000, but I still had kids in college. So, initially, it was a burden. But as I got raises I started, I contributed more, and now am at the full level.

Most people I see are too conservative. A 50-year-old friend of mine has everything in the fixed account, even though he has 15 years to go. That's too conservative.

Name withheld, broadcaster at Voice of America.

Spouse, nurse, retired.

I chose stocks because I knew the money would be there for over 25 years, and over long periods like that, the stock market has always been a winner. I was 45 or 46, probably making $27,000, when I started contributing to the plan. I could easily afford it.

Name withheld, works for the CIA

I'm a registered nurse, but I work part-time with no retirement plan. My husband has a plan at his job, and he's been contributing to it since he was 35. He was earning about $35,000 at that point. It was easiest this way, since we never saw the money. He started contributing 5% of his pay, but later switched to 10%, and because it was pretax, his net income with each paycheck didn't change much. And it's certainly not a burden now. We don't even notice anymore, since we've been doing it for so long.

A lot of people move their money around too much. If possible, they should put in the maximum allowed. Leave it alone and let it grow.

Elizabeth Barnhill, registered nurse. Raised outside Philadelphia, Pennsylvania

Grady Barnhill, works for the Secret Service. Raised in Georgetown, South Carolina

---

I know that the best thing to do is to be aggressive with the money you're not going to use for a lot of years. For long-term investing, you want to be in stocks. If you needed it in three years, that's different. If I don't need it for 20 years, it goes in stocks—and that's why my retirement plan is all in stocks.

I started when I was 25. I was making $13,000. I could easily afford it. And with the company matching my contribution, well, that's a huge incentive. I now contribute 15% of my pay, and I wish I could go to 20% but they won't let me.

As much as I can, I encourage younger people to think about their 401(k). I tell the younger ones to try to get into the habit—like brushing your teeth or combing your hair. But I probably haven't convinced anyone. It's not a priority for the younger set. Beer and movies on Fridays are their priority.

You have to be comfortable with yourself. I couldn't live beyond my means and be comfortable. I know people who spend more of their money now than I do, but they won't be comfortable in retirement. But that's not the way I could live. Still, I do not want to become Silas Marner counting my gold coins. When I have extra money that I don't invest, I use it for worthwhile things, such as helping out friends and family. I want to be comfortable and be able to give to people who can't return it. Just to give to others and have them say "thank you" and smile is wonderful.

I didn't get married when I was real young. Could have done a lot of stupid things if I got married at 19 like my mother, sister, and grandmother.

Name withheld, landscape architect

Spouse, graphic artist

The best advice I can give to anyone starting out in the workplace today is that if they are offered a 401(k) plan at work, get into it the day it is offered. You cannot start too early. I was in the military for eight years and didn't get out until I was 25. I went to work for Sears then, and I jumped at the opportunity to join their 401(k). That was 35 years ago.

Jim Light, insurance agent. Raised in Huntington, West Virginia

---

I started investing in my company retirement plan when I was 39. My salary was $25,000. What I love about the 401(k) is that they take the money before I see it. Had I seen the money, I would have spent it. You live on what you see.

We have never borrowed from the plan. I am strongly opposed to this. But I've seen lots of people do that. There tends to be a "herd mentality" at work—most of the employees tend to listen to each other about how to invest the money they put in the plan. But when I made my decision, I had no idea what the others were doing. I just did what I knew was best.

We started saving outside the plan by sending in $25 a month to a mutual fund. Now that seems like a small amount of money, but it really adds up over time. I would tell people to save like that from day one, no matter what the amount. Just do it and make it your first priority.

Ann, pharmacist

Tom, medical technologist

I keep preaching to my kids to get into the 401(k) as early as possible. They've taken my advice, but they've said it's hard to save when you are young. They are right; it is not easy to save, but you have to do it anyway. In our own life, my wife thought I was crazy to put the maximum amount of money allowable into the 401(k) when we could have used that money for other things, but now, she says she's glad we did it.

Robert Huss, consultant. Raised in Johnstown, Pennsylvania

The best thing to do is be aggressive with the money you're not going to use for a lot of years. If I don't need it for 20 years, it goes in stocks. I've been doing this since I was 25 and earning $13,000 a year.

Wendy Campbell, landscape architect. Raised in Northern Virginia

Duncan Campbell, graphic artist. Raised in Clinton, Iowa

I have never moved the money from stocks in my plan. I am stubborn.

Name withheld, senior engineer

Spouse, retired registered nurse

SECRET #3

Most of Their Wealth Came From Investments That Were Purchased for Less than $1000.

SECRET #3

Most of Their Wealth Came From Investments That Were Purchased for Less than $1000.

"Give me a million dollars, and I'll turn it into two million."

If anything were to ever qualify as a stupid statement, that's the one. Not because the statement is false — but because it is inherently obvious. Anybody can turn a million bucks into two million. The trick is to get that first million![37]

Or how about this one:

"The rich get richer, the poor get poorer."

Many people improperly use this statement as a political weapon—to endorse the idea of taxing the rich and redistributing their wealth to the poor. But giving poor people money doesn't make them rich; if it did, all welfare recipients would be millionaires.

No, this statement is true—but with an entirely different meaning. You see, it contains the secret to accumulating wealth.

The reason rich people get richer and poor people get poorer is that rich people continue to do the things that got them rich in the first place, while poor people continue to do the things that got them poor. So let's try to find out how rich people got that way.

Please, don't say inheritances. That might be how rich people *stay* rich, but that's not how they *got* that way. Go back far enough in the family histories of wealthy Americans and you'll discover that *none of them started out wealthy*. They were all poor—as poor as today's poor.

---

[37] Old Wall Street saying: turning $100 into $1 million is hard work. Turning $1 million into $10 million is inevitable.

Actually, let me restate that. While today's wealthy Americans were once broke, I don't think they were ever really poor. Poor is a state of mind. Broke is a state of wallet. You can fix being broke; it's not so easy to fix being poor.[38]

How do you fix being broke? There's no magic: You just work hard, get a little money, and save some of it. Repeat this process for very long periods of time. Eventually, you won't be broke any more. But the poor person next to you will remain poor—because they will spend any small amounts of money they might come upon, preventing themselves from accumulating any wealth.

If you don't believe this, consider my firm's clients. None of them were born into wealth. As a youth, only 12% were given any money from parents or grandparents, and even then the typical gift was a savings bond, insurance policy, or cash. Only 3% were given stocks as a child. And less than 67% have received any inheritance; of those who did, their inheritance was a small one—33% of those who got an inheritance obtained less than 10% of their wealth this way; only 4% got half or more of their wealth through inheritances.

Also, very few (6%) own businesses, so scratch that as the way to wealth for ordinary Americans. And forget the lottery, too: only 2 of my clients have won, but neither made millions—one won an amount less than 10% of his net worth, while the other says his winnings constitute 11%–20% of his total savings.

Forget insurance as a source, too. Only 6% of our clients have gotten any insurance proceeds at all, and of the 50 respondents who did, only 8 people got half or more of their wealth this way.

---

[38] Besides, it's not true that most rich people owe their wealth to inheritances. The saying "rags to riches to rags in three generations" is largely true. The son of a self-made millionaire might live well, but it is very difficult to preserve wealth much beyond the third generation. Say Granddad builds a net worth of $100 million. He loses half to estate taxes. The other half goes to his three children, who get $17 million each. They each lose half to taxes at their deaths, leaving $2.8 million to each of the nine grandchildren. Clearly, by the fourth generation, there's not much left for the 27 great-grandchildren—unless someone in the family carries on Granddad's tradition and rebuilds the family's wealth. But if they succeed in rebuilding Granddad's wealth through their own hard work, you could hardly label their wealth as coming from "inheritance."

How about a court judgement or lawsuit? Only 12 of our responding clients received money this way, and none of them got much. Five clients got 10% or less of their money in this manner, and none of the remaining seven got more than 50% of their assets this way.

And yet, despite all these "handicaps," our survey respondents have accumulated in savings and investments an average of $500,000. Where did they get it? The answer is simple:

More than 95% obtained their money through their own efforts. They worked hard. Got an education and a good job. Had kids, and worked even harder. Through it all, they managed to save a little money here and there.

And that's all it took.

They didn't begin with $100,000 to invest. Instead, they saved what little money they could scrape together, and they invested it as often as they could. As my clients have shown through our survey, the money they invested was always in small amounts, and usually less than $1,000—often, much less. And yet, investing small amounts was enough to produce wealth for them.

Our survey of successful Americans shows that:

- They began investing when they were young. The average age when they made their first investment was 24; 10% of them started before they were 18.

- They invested small amounts of money. Their initial investment averaged just $658; 24% started with less than $100 while another 22% invested from $100 to $499.

- They invested often. A whopping 92% saved regularly throughout their lives, adding to their savings whenever they could. More than half invested what they had, even though they had less than $1,000; 20% regularly invested amounts of less than $500.

- They invested intelligently. Most—81%—set money aside into a special account earmarked for savings. They'd accumulate a few hundred, and then invest it. Only 4% let money sit at home for any length of time; 96% placed the money first into a savings or checking account, and then transferred the money into stocks and bonds.

- They let nothing stop them from saving. Like all Americans, my clients have experienced a lot of turmoil and change in their lives. But through it all, saving and investing was a constant. According to our survey results, they let little interfere with their savings plans. Although a majority (69%) suffered some circumstance that caused them to temporarily stop saving, only 4% actually let go of the savings habit.

There were lots of reasons my clients interrupted their savings efforts over the course of their lives, and each reason is quite ordinary. But what is most remarkable is how few of my clients allowed these events and circumstances to get them off track. Have you ever blamed your lack of savings on the fact that you've just changed jobs, or relocated to another city, or are buried by college class work, or that you're getting married, or busy raising kids?

Everyone who laments their poverty can offer dozens of reasons why they don't save. My clients faced all these challenges, too, but what sets them apart is that they didn't let these events interfere with their goal to save for the future. For example:

- Almost all went into military service, but only 4% said entering or leaving the military interrupted their savings efforts

- They almost all were married at some point, but only 7% said that changing their marital status interrupted their savings efforts

- Only 8% blamed "some other (nonspecified) event" as the reason why they interrupted their savings efforts

- Only 9% said going to school interrupted their savings efforts

- Only 10% said health problems (personally or within their families) interrupted their savings efforts

- 100% obtained or changed jobs at some point, but only 12% said doing so interrupted their savings efforts

- Although many suffered a job loss or a reduced income, only 15% said such events interrupted their savings efforts

- Everyone moved at least once, but only 21% said changing their place of residence interrupted their savings efforts

- And although almost every respondent has children, less than a third said the cost of raising children interrupted their savings efforts

And the most remarkable statistic of all: Despite all the things that happen to us in life, an incredible 31% said *nothing* ever interrupted their savings efforts. No wonder these people are among the nation's wealthiest Americans.

You can make all the excuses you want, but the fact remains: either you will or you will not achieve wealth. You can make excuses for why you are not saving, or you can move past the excuses and save anyway. You can lament your low pay, your high expenses, your difficult circumstances, or your bad luck. Or you can ignore all those problems and save anyway. It's entirely up to you.

I suspect that one of the most startling discoveries of this research is that my clients accumulated their wealth by investing such small amounts of money. If that surprises you, then you don't understand how money grows. You see, it doesn't take a lot of money to produce wealth. It merely takes a little money—and a lot of time. And although you might not have a lot of money, you certainly do have a lot of time.[39]

---

[39] Worried that you don't have much time left because you're already 50 or 60? Worry not: based on actuarial tables, today's 50-year-olds have a life expectancy of 35 years. Even 60-somethings can expect to live another 20 years. And by the time you reach your 80s, medical science will have figured out a way to keep you going strong into your 100s! So forget the notion that "it's too late." That is simply not true—although it could serve as a dandy excuse to keep you in poverty. By the way, are you poor or merely broke?

Time is all you need to convert small savings into small fortunes. A 20-year-old who saves $45 a month—that's a buck fifty per day—at 12% per year (the stock market's average since 1926), will accumulate nearly $1,000,000 after 45 years. There's hardly a 20-year-old in the country who can't manage to save $1.50 per day—if they want to. And they'll want to once they realize the value of doing so.

But too many don't understand this. They don't realize the impact *time* has on *money*. Oh, sure, we've all heard that "time is money." But few understand what this means. Far too many young Americans—and I'll put everyone under age 45 in this category—don't understand that wealth accumulation is much more a function of time than it is of money.

Few would argue that a 20-year-old is capable of earning and saving $45 a month. If you're 20, I know you're already working or attending college (or both). So what? Is that your excuse for not achieving wealth? Poor people give me sob stories about why they're poor. Broke people don't, because they're too busy overcoming being broke.

Still, there are lots of 20-year-olds who are not currently saving. Just let me get through school, they say, and when I get a job making real money, I'll start to invest. Those already working say they just need to get rid of some bills, or get a raise, or solve a few situations, and then they'll be ready to invest. The result for each case? Whatever your reasons, whatever your excuses[40], you delay saving money.

Forgive me if this seems insensitive. I know what it's like to not have any money, and to struggle to collect what little money you can. Jean and I didn't own a television for four years after we sold ours to pay bills. The money we were earning at the time wasn't nearly enough to pay all our bills, and the Credit Card Shuffle was in full swing.

But none of that matters. After all, if you need $1,500 and you don't have $1,500, it won't matter that you have $1,200 instead of only $1,165—the mess you're in will remain a mess

---

[40] That's all they really are, you know.

either way. But that $45 difference is equal to $1.50 per day. And waiting until you're 21 to begin saving that $1.50 per day means you won't have as much money as the person who started at age 20. That's no surprise. But the amount might be: the difference between how much the 20-year-old accumulates by age 65 and the amount obtained by the 21-year-old is a whopping $109,170.

That's right: the 20-year-old's refusal to save just $1.50 a day ($547.50) for just one year costs her $109,170. More than 11% of the total accumulation from 45 years of savings is secured in just the first year. Lose that year, and you lose that accumulation.

And that's not even the worst part. No, the worst part is this: no matter how hard she tries, no matter how much money she saves in the future, she'll never be able to recoup those lost earnings. Because wealth is produced by time, and once lost, time cannot be recovered.

This is why so many people will put down this book and begin chanting that most common of all financial laments: I Should Have Started Twenty Years Ago.[41] Don't feel bad. Everyone has said this at one time or another. Even the 20-year-olds. Once, after I spoke to a group of high-school sophomores, I overheard a student say to a classmate, "Man! I should've started when I was twelve!"

My point is that there is no value in lamenting the past. Instead, focus your energy on the future—because that is where you are headed, and that is something over which you still have total control. As I noted in Footnote 39, even 60-year-olds have barely completed two thirds of their lives. Fifty-year-olds haven't even reached middle age yet! So instead of lamenting the couldabeens, let's focus on the whereyagoings!

That's what my clients did. They didn't complain about their unfortunate surroundings, background, or circumstances. They didn't expect someone else to solve their problems for them—not their parents, and certainly not the government.

---

[41] And you thought you were the only one!

They simply made the best of their situation. And the one thing they did to assure their wealth: they saved their money. They saved in small amounts, and they saved for a long period of time.

They never had much money, of course. People didn't earn much money in the 1940s, 1950s, and 1960s. And, like you, most of their money was diverted to bills—the rent or mortgage, car payments, food, clothing, and insurance—but still, they managed to scrape together a few dollars here and there. And with this money, they did something uncommon: they invested it.

So start saving money now—no matter how little you have, no matter how old or young you are. And if you think you can't, try these tips, found in my first book, *The Truth About Money*[42]:

1) Save $10 or $25 before you pay this month's bills. Then pay the bills. You'll be broke when you're done (like you are every month), but this way, you'll have saved a few bucks before you went broke.

2) Stop spending coins. By saving your change every month, you'll accumulate $20 or more—literally without trying.

3) Use supermarket coupons, but use them correctly. Next time you use a "Dollar Off" coupon, save that dollar instead of spending it on something else. You should be able to save $20–$50 per month this way.

It won't take long for you to realize how remarkably easy it is to save money. You can do it! Just let my clients show you the way.

---

[42] If I didn't like me so much, I'd sue myself for plagiarism.

SUCCESSFUL INVESTORS:
MOST OF THEIR WEALTH CAME FROM INVESTMENTS THAT WERE PURCHASED FOR LESS THAN $1,000.
"IN THEIR OWN WORDS"

I started saving when I was 38. I'd save about $400 a month, sometimes more. The smallest amount I ever invested was $50. I put this money into stocks via a stockbroker. There was no plan really, other than for me to just keep adding money to my investments. I don't feel as though I had to make sacrifices in order to save, although I certainly faced obstacles—three of them, in fact: I put three kids through college!

Dick Ives, retired Naval Officer. Raised in Wellsville, New York

Pat Ives, secretary. Raised in Spencer, Wisconsin

I began by saving $23 per month. I put this money into mutual funds. I was 24 at the time. It was hard at first, but after it became a habit, it became easy. At this point, we're saving 25% of our salaries, and that includes most of our bonuses. And if we could change the past, we'd increase the amount that we saved.

Dick Amann, proposal writing consultant. Raised in Long Island, New York

Pidge Amann, company president. Raised in Alexandria, Virginia

I started investing when I was 29, just $100 per paycheck. I had to make some sacrifices to do this; I didn't get many of the things other people had, such as cars and furniture. But it's easier than ever now. The smallest amount I ever invested was $25—which I did often—and as my salary increased, so did my savings. I'll probably never stop saving.

Phyllis Parker, Bell Atlantic employee. Raised in West Virginia

Wayne Parker, teacher. Raised in West Virginia

---

§§

We started investing at 35, usually $80 to $100 with each paycheck. We didn't have to make sacrifices to save, but sometimes a bill or two would force us to miss a monthly investment. But we don't save anymore. We're now retired and enjoying the savings!

We bought Exxon stock, and kept on buying until we owned 100 shares. It then split to 200 shares, then split a couple more times. Some 14 years later, we had a considerable amount of money.

Max Thomas, retired Army Officer, and now consultant. Raised in Indiana

Dennisse Thomas, registered nurse and housewife. Raised in Indiana

---

§§

I started saving when I was 17. Every two months, I'd buy a U.S. Savings Bond for $18.75. I got the money from my paycheck. I wasn't saving for anything in particular—just for a "rainy day." Then, as my income increased, so did my savings.

In 1950, we started buying AT&T stock—just one to three shares at a time. It's now worth about $600,000. If I

could, I'd go back in time and buy fewer consumer items—
and more stock!

*Kathryn Coleman, President/CEO of a credit union, retired. Raised
in Alexandria, Virginia*

*Vic Coleman, telephone company plant supervisor, retired. Raised in
Pittsburgh, Pennsylvania*

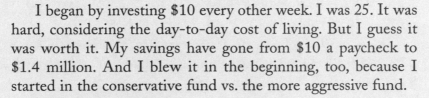

I began by investing $10 every other week. I was 25. It was
hard, considering the day-to-day cost of living. But I guess it
was worth it. My savings have gone from $10 a paycheck to
$1.4 million. And I blew it in the beginning, too, because I
started in the conservative fund vs. the more aggressive fund.

Name withheld, homemaker

Spouse, project manager

We started investing at age 28, just $1,000 or $2,000 a year.
There was no plan, really. We just put this money into stocks.
It wasn't hard—we just made up our minds and did it.

Jody Pearce, housewife. Raised in Pennsylvania

Don Pearce, construction. Raised in Pennsylvania

I saved $165 from each paycheck, back when I was 30. I put
that money into General Electric stock, a mutual fund, and
U.S. Savings Bonds. There was no particular plan; I just saw it
as an opportunity to save some money and decided to take full

advantage of it. There were some sacrifices I had to make. We gave up the purchase of a lot of material goods. But it was worth it—that GE stock is now worth a quarter of a million dollars.

Name withheld, computer systems manager

Spouse, manager of operations

I started out by saving $25 to $50 with each paycheck. I was only 23. It was easy. I don't think we'll ever stop saving.

In early 1970s, I bought four shares of Marriott stock for $74. Now it has turned into about 120 shares of stock, worth $3,000. Not bad for a $74 investment.

Name withheld, business automation consultant

Spouse, law enforcement

I was 24 when I started to save. We'd invest $25 a month. It was easy to save, because we didn't spend much. If we didn't have the cash, we didn't buy anything.

Marian Kilgore, retired teacher. Raised in Washington, Pennsylvania

George Kilgore, retired mechanic. Raised in London, Ohio

Starting about age 30, I'd invest $700 per month. I first bought savings bonds, and later, mutual funds. I had no real organized plan. I just saved every month.

Kathleen Keim, international economist. Raised in Milwaukee, Wisconsin

At 35, I started investing $50 a month, then worked up to $300 to $400 a month as my salary grew. I didn't have a formal plan, just knew that I needed to have some long-term savings.

Jim McDaniel, park manager. Raised in Boston, Massachusetts

Michele McDaniel, administrative assistant. Raised in Lowell, Massachusetts

I used to invest $10 to $15 a month into mutual funds. I was 28. I once bought a stock over time, invested a total of $1,300. It's now worth $11,000.

Name withheld, director of administrative services, retired

Spouse, secretary, retired

We started investing as newlyweds, when we were 25, just $15 with each paycheck. That's the best advice we can give—start saving as soon as you can in life, and get used to doing it.

Darlene Joyce, underwriter. Raised in Cleveland, Ohio

Michael Joyce, systems engineer. Raised in Cleveland, Ohio

I started investing when I was 35, about $100 a month. There wasn't a real plan like we "had" to save. It was a matter of just saving money and letting it accumulate. As time went by and salaries increased, we increased our monthly savings whenever possible.

Carol Wyant, program analyst. Raised in Beltsville, Maryland

Dan Wyant, biologist. Raised in Camp Springs, Maryland

I am not successful at buying and selling stocks . . . I tend to buy and sell at the wrong time. Very early on I learned it is better to invest and then forget about it, and let the professionals take care of it. I invested a small chunk of money ($15K in 1965) in a mutual fund and let it go at that. That investment today is worth three quarters of a million dollars. I never added anything to it . . . it was all compounded earnings.

L.B., retired. Raised in Washington, DC

My father invested $2,500 in mutual funds in 1966, and 28 years later, it was worth around $66,000.

Larry Gallion, retired U.S. Navy. Raised throughout the U.S. and overseas

---

I started by setting up a monthly allotment to invest $50, but I couldn't handle that. So I changed it to $50 each quarter instead of monthly. But I always kept sending something regularly. And I increased the amount, and eventually went back to monthly, as my salary increased.

I never "scored big" on a stock or anything like that. Not that that matters—anybody who sets up a program where they save automatically like I did will do incredibly well. After a few years has gone by, you'll find it to have become a significant amount of money.

It's just amazing that the one thing that works best for you is time.

Name withheld, international sales
Spouse, housewife

I bought mutual funds when I was 22. I invested $50 month for about eleven years. On occasion I would invest $1,000 to $2,000 into IRAs or individual stocks. I never really missed the money.

I once invested $300 into some mutual funds for each of my children. After 16 years, the accounts grew to about $3,000.

Back when the market crashed in 1987, I sold some investments and bought tax-free bonds. I know now I should have held onto the investments and rode the crash out.

Name withheld, IRS Employee

Spouse, homemaker

I was in the Army at age 18, and I sent money to my mother every month, which she invested for me. After the Army, I completed undergraduate school and then pharmacy school. I decided to take an economics course. When I asked my economics professor how to read the stock pages, he couldn't tell me.

Lawrence Jones, retired pharmacist. Raised in Pine Bluff, Arkansas

Sarah S. Jones, supervisor. Raised in Windsor, North Carolina

---

I was 24 when I started investing. I invested $10 per paycheck on a regular basis.

Paul M. Marriott, Jr., civil engineering designer. Raised in Cumberland, Maryland

Barbara Marriott, housewife, former schoolteacher. Raised in Cumberland, Maryland

I started investing when I was 22, by putting aside money from my paycheck. I did that every two weeks for 38 years. I began with just five dollars, and every time I got a promotion or raise, I put half in savings and half toward improving my standard of living.

I invested in real estate and mutual funds, as well as some individual stocks, and we reinvested all the dividends and capital gains. I invest the maximum I can, and we maintain a "don't touch" policy with savings.

Gary H. Bullis, engineer. Raised in Graham, North Carolina

Linda Bullis, homemaker—and the household's bookkeeper. Raised in Scranton, Kansas

SECRET #4

They Rarely Move From One Investment to Another.

SECRET #4
They Rarely Move From One Investment to Another.

My clients are living proof that you can achieve remarkable success by saving just small amounts of money. But where should you save it?

Most people believe investment success depends on three things: your ability to invest large amounts of money (the rich get richer syndrome), your ability to get big, quick returns, and your ability to actively manage your assets to maximize your profits. We've already destroyed the first two myths. Let's now dispel the last.

Broadly speaking, there are only two ways to manage money, loosely defined as "buy-and-hold" and "market timing." The first has you buy a variety of quality investments (using diversification) and hold onto them for long periods of time.

The second approach disagrees with this. Market timers concede that buy-and-holders do enjoy long-term gains from their strategy, but they also claim that buy-and-holders suffer substantially from volatility. Wouldn't it be better if you rode the "up" markets but avoided the "down" markets? Market timers claim that their method would bring you two big benefits: you'd enjoy lower risk (by avoiding the sharp declines that accompany the stock market) along with greater wealth.

Everyone agrees that the principle behind market timing makes sense. Consider two investors, each of whom puts $10,000 into the stock market in 1927. Investor One holds his stocks for 71 years. As of December 31, 1998, his $10,000 has grown in value to $21 million, which represents a 13.4% average annual return.

Investor Two, however, does not turn his back on his investment. Instead, he watches carefully, and with great skill he anticipates when stocks are about to lose money, and before each downturn occurs, he efficiently sells his stocks to preserve the value of his account. He then keeps his money in cash, earning interest at the annual rate of 5%, and does not venture back into stocks until they are about to rise in value from their current levels. He does this—getting out just before the market goes down, or getting in just before the market goes up—for 71 years. The value of his account as of December 31, 1998: $54 *trillion.*

Clearly, market timing produces wealth far in excess of buying-and-holding. The only problem: Investor Two doesn't exist. His story is pure fiction, offered to you merely to demonstrate that market-timing's proponents[43] can easily concoct fabulous stories about how you, too, can create wealth.[44]

Although Investor Two doesn't exist, Investor One does. Who is Investor One? My firm's clients—and there are many others like them. According to my research, my firm's clients achieved their wealth in a very specific way: they buy investments and they hold onto them for long periods.

I asked my firm's clients about their trading habits, both for 1998 and for the five years ending December 31, 1998. You'll recall that 1998 was an extremely volatile year—one of the most volatile on record. The Dow Jones Industrial Average gained 17.2% from January 1 to July 17. It then lost 16% from July 17 to September 30. This period included a spectacular 502-point drop in a single day (August 31), the worst daily decline since the Crash of 1987. Stocks then rebounded 20.3% from October 1 through the end of the year. If ever there was an opportunity—or an incentive—to engage in market timing, 1998 was it.

And yet, when asked, "How many times did you move money from one mutual fund to another in 1998?," 52% of my firm's clients said they never made a single change to their

---

[43] Read: market-timing newsletter editors who want you to subscribe to their publications, authors of market-timing books who want you to buy their books, motivational speakers who want you to pay their seminar tuition, and market-timing investment advisors who want you to hire them to manage your assets (for a fee, of course).
[44] Give these guys your money, and wealth certainly will be created, all right—theirs!

portfolio the entire year. Another 43% made one or two changes, but this can be dismissed as routine portfolio adjustments, not market-timing attempts.[45] Only 4% of clients moved money four to six times in 1998, and just one fellow out of our entire surveyed client base made 12+ moves.

Similar results were obtained when we asked about our clients' actions over the past five years. With a longer time span, you'd naturally expect to see a somewhat greater incidence of movement between mutual funds—especially considering that this time period included the infamous 1994, one of the worst performing years in Wall Street history. The chart below shows the market's volatility since January 1, 1994. With the benefit of hindsight, we can see many opportunities to engage in market timing. And yet, throughout this entire five-year period, 85% of my firm's clients made three or fewer moves in their portfolios; 22% made absolutely no changes at all! And again, only one poor soul made more than 12 moves.

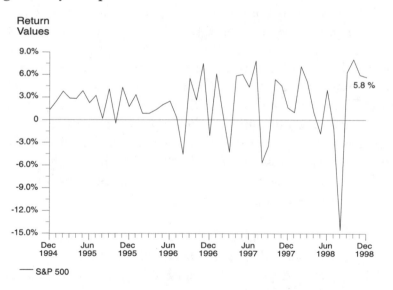

---

[45] I know this because these people are my clients, and we handled the transactions for them. We periodically rebalance our clients' portfolios, for example, and this exercise is done regardless of current market activity. Other clients, such as those preparing to enter retirement, needed to make changes in their portfolios so we could begin sending them a monthly income from their investments. Bottom line: making one or two changes in a portfolio during a year is prudent management, not market timing.

Clearly, successful Americans achieve wealth by buying investments and then leaving them alone for very long periods. By contrast, I have never seen a single documented case of anyone who has created wealth through market timing.

I stressed the folly of market timing very clearly in both of my previous books, so I won't belabor the point here.[46] No, the point I want to make here is that most investors today completely agree with me. They tell me they prefer the buy-and-hold approach and that they believe market timing to be foolish, and they are quick to say that they do not engage in this frivolous and pointless activity.

Do you agree with them?

I'm certain you do. If I were to ask you whether you're a market timer or a buy-and-holder, I'm certain you would tell me that you believe market timing is dangerous, and that you manage your money consistent with the concepts of the buy-and-hold strategy.

By the way, most of the people who tell me this are liars.

Forgive me. It's not polite to call people liars. But it's the truth. You see, people will tell me that they agree with the buy-and-hold method, and that they understand that people who try to time the market are virtually certain to lose money in the effort. They know this, because they've read one of my previous books, and saw the statistics showing that successful market timing is virtually impossible, or because they've tried it and, like virtually all market timers, they've failed miserably.

In my earlier books, I demonstrated why market timers are doomed to failure. Some of the examples I cited:

a) For the five years ended December 31, 1997, the stock market gained 24.6%. This entire profit was produced in just 40 days. Would you be able to predict which days they were?

---

[46] Although I do encourage you to read the books' relevant chapters if you aren't convinced that market timing is merely hype.

b) In the 864 months between 1926 and 1997, where stocks averaged 10.4% per year, 61% of those months were profitable. Yet, if you took away the top 72 months—just 8% of the total—your total return would have been zero. Removing 8% of the time eliminates 100% of the profits.

c) The Federal Reserve Board's own economic forecasts are never correct. Considering that the Fed controls interest rates, you'd think they should be able to influence the very events they're trying to predict. Yet, in 14 years, the Fed's own predictions of Gross Domestic Product resulted in a 100% error rate.

d) Even at the U.S. Trading and Investing Championships, where top professionals trade real money (their own), few succeed. Of 3,500 entries in one series of contests, only 22% of entrants made any money at all. Only a handful managed to keep pace with or exceed the S&P 500.

Some people either ignored or were unaware of these problems with market timing, and thus tried to do it themselves. The results were uniformly terrible. They got out when they should have stayed in, or they stayed in when they should have gotten out. On top of that, they incurred taxes and transaction costs in the process, further eroding their returns.

So there is no doubt that you agree with me that nothing beats the buy-and-hold strategy. Why, then, do I accuse you of being a liar?

Because your actions are not matching your words.

Often, when I'm meeting with a new client, the client will tell me about their financial goals. College planning for their kids is often a key goal, and retirement for themselves always is. Indeed, if you're like most people, securing your own retirement is your primary financial goal. And if you're like most parents of school-age children, paying for college also is a high priority.

Later in this first meeting, after we've reviewed their current assets and considered their ability to save further, I pop the question.

"Is it your intention to leave this money invested until the child reaches college, or until you retire?"

Without exception, they answer, "Yes."

And, so, I develop a complete set of financial recommendations for them. We review them in a second (and sometimes, third) meeting. I explain to my clients everything about the proposed investments in great detail. I stress that these investment recommendations are based on the premise that they will hold these investments for many years, that market timing strategies will not be used. The client acknowledges all this. The client then asks lots of questions. These questions show that the client has indeed been listening, for the questions are thoughtful and well considered. I answer each question thoroughly, and the meeting continues until both the client and I are satisfied that they fully understand everything they need to know. Then, and only then, do I tell them that I will mail the paperwork to them so they can open their accounts.

And that's when they say it.

"*Ric, we like the work you've done. Everything looks good, and we have no doubt that we're going to proceed. But...*"

Here it comes.

"*...We're just a little concerned about [insert economic, political, or social crisis here], and so, we wonder if it might be best to just wait a few weeks, just to see how this thing will shake out?*"

And the truth comes out. They're market timers.

"*Oh, no, we're not!*" They protest. "*We're in this for the long haul! Really! It's just that [insert economic, political, or social crisis here] is going on, and, well, the [stock/bond/real estate/gold] market looks a little shaky at the moment. Wouldn't it make sense to wait just a week or two to see how things get resolved?*"

They're not market timers, you understand. They just want to see what happens in the market before they invest. They're not market timers, you understand. They just want to wait a short time before they invest. But they're not market timers, you understand.

Yeah, I understand the situation *completely*.

You see, confronted with all the academic data proving that market timing doesn't work, people don't like to admit that that's what they are doing. No one wants to admit it—to themselves, let alone to you. If asked, they'll deny it. Yet, they insist on acting just like a market timer. They'll even deny it while they're doing it.[47]

You see, people don't engage in market timing because they have studied a stock's fundamentals and are convinced that now is the time to do this or that. Nor are they technical analysts, plotting the charts to conclude that now is the time to do this or that. Neither are they quantitative theorists, searching for data points with their computer models to see if now is the time to do that or this. No, these people are merely acting on their emotions, making investment decisions based on their feelings. If they feel fear, they want to get out—or stay out—of the market, and if they feel greed, they want to get in, or stay in.[48]

Indeed, emotions are the cause of most investment failures. This failure can be explained in two ways: symptoms and causes. The symptoms of emotional investing are easily seen. People fret over current events. They fear that today's headlines are going to result in a collapse of the entire global economic system, and this fear keeps them from investing. Or they envision that the latest news will translate into huge profits for the markets, so they can't wait to get in.

In 1999, there was a lot to worry about. El Niño/La Niña wreaked economic and human havoc around the world; Japan, Russia, and Brazil were still suffering severe economic turmoil; Iraq and Kosovo required U.S. military action; the president's scandal didn't want to go away; and of course, let's not forget Y2K. For all these reasons, many people did not want to put or keep their money in the stock market.

---

[47] I'm not an alcoholic, he said while drinking a beer. And I can quit smoking anytime I want, she said while lighting another cigarette.

[48] Not that this matters much. Because even those timers who are fundamentalists, technicians, or quants fail at timing anyway.

At the same time, internet stocks skyrocketed, gaining 1,000% and more. Inflation and interest rates were at their lowest levels in years, creating the biggest real estate boom in 20 years. Drug companies introduced some of the greatest solutions to serious medical conditions in decades—and reaped huge profits along the way. Unemployment was at its lowest level in years. And, of course, the stock market was enjoying record levels. For all these reasons, many people insisted on placing all their money into stocks.

Both groups of people were making critical investment decisions based largely, if not solely, on their emotions. As soon as their sentiments changed, both groups of people would want to switch to the other side, taking their investments with them. In other words, they're engaging in the practice of market timing—but they'll deny it if asked. *"I'm in it for the long haul."* They'll say. *"It's just that, for right now . . ."* and so it goes with them.

These are the symptoms of emotional investing. They are easy to spot, and fortunately, sometimes easy to stop. Sometimes, I can get my clients to stop acting like market timers merely by showing them that they're acting this way. Often, people who are acting as market timers truly don't know that's what they're doing; they honestly don't know that wanting to wait and see how the impeachment trial would end before investing is a form of market timing, that wanting to learn the results of some arms negotiation in the Middle East is, indeed, market timing. Many people think market timers move in and out of the market several times an hour or day.[49] They don't know that timers might simply be people who delay investing or who sell investments because of current events, or people who want to move all they've got into the market *now* because of all the perceived profits there—and once you point this out to them, they quickly see their error, and they stop their destructive behavior.

---

[49] That's not market timing. That's day trading, an extreme form of timing. If only fools try to engage in timing, day traders must be true idiots.

But sometimes, the symptoms are not so easy to kill. Often, people act with their money the way they do because of deep emotional issues. Psychologists have long studied how emotions cause people to act certain ways, but only recently has this been applied to money. It has resulted in the creation of a new field called behavioral finance, which is providing fascinating insights about how people handle their personal finances.

Much of this work is credited to Daniel Kahnemann of Princeton University and Amos Tversky of Stanford, who created the field some 20 years ago. The University of Chicago's Richard Thaler is perhaps today's leading proponent of behavioral finance, largely thanks to his 1992 book, *The Winner's Curse*.

In the section that follows, let me share with you some of the results of this new research. As you read about the psychological mistakes people make, and as you see yourself within its pages, keep one thing in mind: successful investors don't make these mistakes.

SUCCESSFUL INVESTORS:
THEY RARELY MOVE FROM ONE INVESTMENT TO ANOTHER.
" IN THEIR OWN WORDS "

I've owned each of my current investments for about seven years. Two of them, I've owned for about 30 years. That's the proper approach, in my opinion: buy them and hold onto them forever.

The last time I made a change was about a year ago. I moved from one investment to another because the current one's outlook wasn't as good as I had liked. Before that, the most recent change I made occurred three years ago. I could move around more, but I don't want to be bothered with it. I'm not interested in doing research or "playing the market."

When I buy investments, I tend to hold onto them for more than 10 years, and I never move them around. The most recent change was five years ago. If you invest wisely and carefully, you shouldn't need to make many changes.

Name withheld, bookkeeper

Spouse, retired V.P. of supply company

I've been investing for a long time. I tend to hold my investments for 10 to 15 years, one of them I've held for about 20 years.

Lillian Brown, adjunct professor at Georgetown University. Raised in Huntsville, Ohio

I intend to own my investments indefinitely—at least 15 to 20 years. I move them rarely.

The last time I made a change was 2½ years ago: I owned a small life insurance policy that had a cash surrender value that was greater than the death benefit. It was clear to cash it in and invest that money into a variable annuity. Before that, my most recent change was nearly nine years ago. I was rolling over retirement benefits and consolidating smaller investments.

Too many investors don't always consider the long-range effects of moving money. They often think of getting out of stocks when the market doesn't look good. Over time, this is dangerous.

Name withheld, human resources professional

I've owned my investments for more than ten years. I don't really ever move them.

Jovita Franco, sales representative. Raised in Manila, Philippines

Don Franco, veterinarian. Raised in Trinidad, West Indies

Once I buy investments, I keep them a minimum of five years. I buy them to hold, not to change them. Before you act, you should talk with a financial advisor to make sure you know what you're doing.

Joseph Rogers, manufacturing coordinator. Raised in Louisa, Virginia

Edna Rogers, secretary. Raised in Demarest, New Jersey

We move investments around very little. By sticking in through the ups and downs, we can achieve long term profits while avoiding excessive fees.

Ernie Hubbard, engineer. Raised near Fayetteville, North Carolina

Jeanne Hubbard, real estate sales assistant. Raised in Crookston, Minnesota

---

I rarely sell investments. The last time was strictly for tax purposes: Even though I had made money with a mutual fund, I actually had a taxable loss because of all the dividend reinvestments. So I was able to sell the fund, earn a profit, and still get a tax deduction. And then I reinvested my money into another, similar investment, which allowed me to stay fully invested. Talk about having your cake and eating it too!

Name withheld, systems manager

Spouse, retired secretary

Good personal experience has reinforced the wisdom of sticking with one's investments for the long term. My belief is that those who move money from one investment to another are motivated by fear or greed. I take advantage of dollar cost averaging and compound interest with a sound, diverse portfolio created to meet my needs by a financial planner. I plan to stay the course.

Barbara Ramee, travel accounting administrator. Raised in Meriden, Connecticut

I have owned my current investments for the past 15 years. I don't move money around unless my financial advisor recommends it, which is rare. In fact, my most recent change was three years ago. I call this "benign neglect." The investments are being watched closely, but that doesn't mean changes must be made.

I have always believed in "buying and holding." If someone wanted to move money around, I would ask them if they knew enough about the advantages and disadvantages about making that move. And on whose advice were they relying?

Vivian Rosskamm, teacher trainer. Raised in suburban Maryland

---

We own our investments for long periods. We like to hold them indefinitely. The more you move money, the more expenses you'll incur. Before you move something, try to identify what your objective is. Often, moving the money doesn't help you reach your objective.

Ginny Geiling, part owner of a contractor company. Raised in Mamaroneck, New York

John Geiling, V.P. of marketing. Raised in Pineville, Louisiana

---

I have owned my stocks up to 20 years; my mutual funds for 10 to 15 years. I move my investments rarely. For example, my most recent change was 18 months ago, merely to create a more diversified portfolio. I don't spend time paying attention to investments. So I just leave the money alone for long periods of time untouched. Now that I'm working with a financial advisor, I now work on developing a more diversified portfolio.

People tend to sell their investments too soon. You must be very cautious about moving your money around.

Richard W. Voelker, research scientist. Raised in Plainview, Nebraska

Rella S. Voelker, housewife. Raised in Mill Creek, West Virginia

---

I keep my investments as is for long periods. I've owned each of my current investments for five years, for example.

Richard Six, aerospace and electronics. Raised in Miami, Florida

---

Except for a few investments, I've held all my investments for about five years, some for as much as seven years. The last time I sold anything was 18 months ago. Before that, I hadn't sold anything for at least four to five years.

Probably the smartest thing I've ever done was to hold my investments longer than one would think you should hold it.

George Gentili, lawyer. Raised in Summit, Illinois

Gail Gentili, schoolteacher. Raised in Willow Springs, Illinois

---

Our focus is long-term, and I don't plan on selling investments once I buy them. I try to hold onto them for five to ten years at a minimum.

John Thune, retired engineer. Raised in Green Bay, Wisconsin

Betsy Thune, retired manager of research. Raised in Long Island, New York

The amount of time I hold investments depends on the investment, but looking back on average, I'd say I tend to own investments for five to eight years. The last time I made a change was three years ago; before that, five to six years ago. But you have to have your ear to the ground and watch your investments the whole time. Just because you don't sell them doesn't mean you don't watch them.

Name withheld, chemist

Spouse, librarian

I like to own mutual funds for three to four years at a minimum. The only thing I change is the asset allocation; my fund changes reflect changes in the allocation. If you have an asset allocation model, you aren't inclined to move money from investment to investment very often. If you buy quality products, then you should be able to keep your money invested, then just wait and see what happens.

I understand that I'm very good at making money (and spending it too!) but that doesn't mean I'm good at knowing how to invest it. As a matter of fact, I'm inclined to think that the instincts that are appropriate for running a business, such as opportunism and responsiveness to changing conditions, are inappropriate for successful investing. For that's why I rely on professional advice.

Phil Wright, business owner, and sales and marketing executive. Raised in Iowa

Suzanne Wright, housewife. Raised in Iowa

I try to own my investments for the long-term, 10 years or more. Generally speaking, from my perspective, the longer you hold money in a fund, the better you can do. If you move money around all the time, you're trying to outguess the market and I don't know if you can do that.

Hank Baker, engineer. Raised in Lucinda, Pennsylvania

Betty Baker, retired nurse. Raised in Broackway, Pennsylvania

———————————— ∬ ————————————

Once we buy them, we keep them.

Susan Clapper, part-time office manager. Raised in the military— an "Army brat"

James Clapper, senior consultant. Raised in the military—another "Army brat"

———————————— ∬ ————————————

I don't really set a time frame, but I've owned most of my current investments about five years. I really don't think it's necessary to move money around more than that. I mean, I could move it around everyday and drive myself crazy, but I prefer to let it sit. I'd rather just let my money ride and grow with a long-term perspective. The smartest thing I ever did was to open my eyes to the world of the market and to see what it has to offer. I've always had an interest in Wall Street, and I've even been on the floor of the New York Stock Exchange.

Barbara J. Haugh, staff associate at a brokerage firm. Raised in Toledo, Ohio

———————————— ∬ ————————————

I don't think you accomplish anything by jumping around. I think people move around based upon past performance, which doesn't mean anything.

Name withheld, accountant. Raised in Cincinnati, Ohio

Spouse, housewife

I try to hold my investments a pretty long time, at least 10 years. My most recent change was three years ago. Market timing doesn't work. If you're in good investments and your portfolio is balanced properly, stick it out through the tough times and don't watch the price of your investments every day. Looking back, I've found that the investments that I left alone did the best over the long term.

John Kirzl, program manager. Raised in New York, New York

Marie Kirzl, housewife, part-time art instructor. Raised in Brooklyn, New York

---

You'll be better off if you just let your money sit. And don't forget to give to charity and help those who are needy.

Rosemary Daily, schoolteacher and homemaker. Raised in Philippi, West Virginia

Tom Daily, engineer. Raised in Arlington, Washington, DC

mind
over
money

Why Investors Make
the Mistakes They Do

mind over money

Why Investors Make the Mistakes They Do

Studies in behavioral finance demonstrate that people make big mistakes with their money, and the purpose of this academic field is to study what you're doing wrong in order to help you overcome your mistakes.

In this section, we'll examine nine of what I consider to be the most important—and widespread—psychological issues that cause investors to make mistakes. What is perhaps most important for you to understand is that most people who fail financially are set up to do so even before they make their first financial decision. By bringing emotional baggage to economic decisions, they set themselves up for failure, usually without even knowing it. And then, when they do fail, they can't figure out why. In this section of the book, you're going to learn some of the reasons why people make bad decisions.

There is little debate that people act emotionally when they make financial decisions. Therefore, let's look first at the two most powerful emotions pertaining to money: fear and greed.

Fear

Fear is defined here as a *lack of confidence in the market*. The reason many people don't like to invest in stocks is because they're afraid that the stock market might crash. Now, everyone knows that stock markets don't crash for no reason. Instead, market crashes are caused by major national or international problems. Thus, those who fear market crashes are really worried about some major economic, political, or social event that's taking place (or which *might* take place). We've already talked about some of things that were worrying investors in 1999, for example (El Niño/La Niña, economic woes in Japan, Russia, and Brazil; political unrest in Iraq and Kosovo; the White House scandal; and Y2K). What we must do to quell these fears is to see if these problems might indeed cause the stock market to crash.

The way to do this is to *test the hypothesis*. Yet, too few fear-filled people do this; most do not try to prove or disprove the basis for their fear. For example, many people who fear snakes think snakes are slimy. These phobics won't touch a snake to see if their theory is true, they don't ask anyone or read any literature about snakes to see if it's true, and because they are so certain of their thesis, they refuse to touch a snake even when offered the opportunity to do so. Thus, many who fear snakes firmly believe that snakeskin is slimy, even though it's not. The irony is that, sometimes, learning the truth is enough to help people overcome their fear of snakes.

Likewise, many financial fears are merely untested theories. Of course they're untested, these phobics will say—you can't prove that a future event won't cause a market crash—and this position lets them claim that their fears are justified. But what these people fail to consider is that the events they fear (or others like them) have already occurred. So let's examine history to see if fears of a market crash are rational fears.[50]

As I demonstrated in *The Truth About Money*[51], humans are always in the midst of a severe economic or political crisis. And yet, in the 58 years since 1940, stocks have risen 77% of the time anyway. Are the problems of today any worse than those of the past? Consider how you'd feel about investing in stocks:

---

[50] And before we go any further, let's focus on the word *rational*. Indeed, some fears are very rational. If you saw a tiger running straight for you, you'd be quite rational to be scared. But if a steel fence stood between the tiger and you, fear of an attack would be irrational. To succeed financially, you must act on rational thinking and avoid acting on irrational thinking.
[51] 650 pages, 130 charts and graphs, 88 cartoons, and 90 famous quotes—all for just $24.95. Order five while they last!

- If the president, one of the most popular in history, were to die in office

- If the nation suddenly faced extreme labor unrest

- If tensions with a powerful foreign country grew to the point that there was talk of war

- If a foreign country with known anti-American sentiments suddenly exploded a nuclear bomb

- If the U.S. military sent tens of thousands of soldiers into battle, and

- If Congress held hearings on the private lives of thousands of Americans

Such a scenario is at least as discomforting, certainly, as the worries we face today. Many people would consider such a scenario to be a dangerous time to invest.

And yet it was quite profitable. For indeed, all the above events actually occurred, in a 10-year period from 1945 to 1954. During this time:

- President Franklin Roosevelt, perhaps the most beloved president in U.S. history, dies in office. (1945)

- The rise of labor unions leads to extreme labor-management problems, often with violent results. (1946)

- The Cold War begins (1947)

- Russia detonates its first Atomic Bomb (1949)

- The Korean Conflict begins, with thousands of U.S. troops deployed (1950)

- The U.S. Government seizes mills (1952)

- Russia detonates its first Hydrogen Bomb (1953)

- The McCarthy Hearings are held (1954)

And yet, during this 10-year period, stocks rose at an average annual rate of 18.4%. Only twice during these 10 years did stocks fail to make money (in 1946, when stocks fell 8%, and in 1953, when stocks lost less than 1%). Clearly, people continued to buy corn flakes in spite of the Soviet threat. While people built bomb shelters, America continued to prosper.

But people who fear the market will turn this history lesson on its head. They point to data showing that stocks do indeed drop a great deal in a short period—especially during crises. And they are correct: on average, in the past, the stock market has fallen an average of 16% in the five weeks following some major economic, political, or social event. But what fearful people fail to acknowledge is that, in the six months following those declines, the stock market climbed 15%, and was up 22% within one year after each crisis. So, yes, a crisis can cause stocks to fall, but that does not mean stocks don't recover.

A great example of this occurred in 1998. Stocks rose 17.2% from January 1 through July 17. Prices then fell sharply, with stocks falling 16% from July 17 through September 30. But from October 1 to the end of the year, stocks regained 20.3%, ending the year with a profit of 28%.

Thus, throughout history, we have experienced many crises. Yet the world goes on. But what if it doesn't? What if the *next* crisis is "the big one"—the one that truly destroys us?

Then you might as well invest in stocks. Because if Russia does drop that bomb on us, it won't have mattered where you invested. But if that bomb never explodes, you'll wish you had some of your money in stocks. In other words, if you're right—and the end is near—it doesn't matter what you do. But if you're wrong—and the world survives—you'll wish you had money in the stock market.

Another reason people fear stocks is because they know stock prices are very volatile. And their version of history supports this position: since 1926 (876 months), stocks made money only 60% of the time. That's not very reassuring to ordinary consumers.

But I would argue that this view of history is incorrect. Do you measure your trip across country in inches—or in miles? People who look at the daily and monthly performance of the market are certain to feel that stocks are volatile—because, in short periods, they are. But over long periods, the stock market is not volatile at all. Indeed, in every 15- and 20-year rolling interval since 1926, the stock market has made money. That's right: the stock market was profitable 100% of the time. On top of that, 90% of the gains ranged from 6% to 17% per year. Thus, the real question is "how much money will stocks make?" rather that worrying whether stocks will make money at all.

Examine history. It'll help you overcome your fear. But be careful *how* you study history, because too close a look can hurt you. Indeed, a series of experiments conducted by Dr. Thaler and his colleagues in 1995 and 1996 demonstrated that the more closely you watch the markets, the more distorted your view of it.

In the experiment, Thaler had each of his students create a portfolio of stocks and bonds. The students then sat before computer screens for an hour, during which time they were shown how the markets performed over a given 25-year period. Some students were given about 200 market updates—one for each six week interval over the 25 years—while others received only five updates—one for each 5-year interval.

After receiving this information, the students were asked to create a new portfolio, one that would be held for the next 40 years. Results: the group of students that had received frequent market updates allocated 40% of their portfolios to stocks, while those who had received only five updates placed 66% of their money into stocks.

Clearly, the more closely you watch the markets, the less confident you are in them. If you doubt this, everyone who fears the market will tell you the same thing: they've never studied the 20-year record of stocks, but they always hear about the Dow on the evening news. And the daily gyrations frighten them—even to the point of keeping them out of the market.

Another way to overcome your fear of stocks is to convert those fears into numbers. This is especially important if you are worried that the market is too high right now. With the stock market at an all-time high (at this writing), it's a common concern, and it leads many people to fret that this is not a good time to invest.

So let me ask you two questions:

1) Based on the current level of the Dow Jones Industrial Average (11,000 at this writing), what do you guess will be the level of the Dow in 20 years?

    Your answer is: _____

2) What do you guess will be the stock market's average annual return over the next 20 years?

    Your answer is: _____

Understandably, many people have difficulty answering these questions—especially the second one. Therefore, to help you arrive at a prediction, consider the following data:

- Since 1926, the average annual return of the stock market, as measured by the S&P 500 Stock Index, has been 12% per year.
- Since 1982, the average annual return has been 15% per year.
- Since 1993, the average annual return has been 25% per year.

So, with the benefit of this information, let's ask that last question again:

    What do you guess will be the stock market's average annual return over the next 20 years?

    Your answer is: _____

Did your answer change? For most people, it does. Which of your two answers do you believe will prove to be more accurate—your first guess, or your second one? Most people place more confidence in their second answer, because it was obtained with the benefit of statistical data—demonstrating that studying the market enables you to feel more confident about your abilities (and hence, more comfortable about stocks).

Now that you have a confident prediction, let's give you the opportunity to change the answer you gave to the first question:

> Based on the current level of the Dow Jones Industrial Average (11,000 at this writing), what do you guess will be the level of the Dow in 20 years?

Your answer is: _____

After going through this process in my seminars, I find that most participants change their guess of the Dow's future average annual return, but many leave unchanged their prediction of the Dow's future level (most of those who do change it, do so only slightly). This means most people consider themselves better at predicting the future Dow than they do at calculating average annual rates of return. After all, you know about the stock market, while the latter is merely a math puzzle.[52]

Based on my experience in seminars, I'm willing to bet that you predicted that the Dow's average annual return will be between 10% and 15%. I say this because 80% of my audiences feel this way. There are always a few who believe the market will produce a huge number—25% or more—and there are sometimes a handful who offer predictions of 7% or 8%. But I

---

[52] And we all hate math!

rarely encounter someone who predicts a return as low as 5%, and I've never met a soul who said that the stock market will produce a negative number.[53]

Let's see where the Dow would be in 20 years if it did indeed produce the average annual returns that most people say it will produce:

- If the Dow earns just 7% per year over the next 20 years, the Dow will be 44,000.

- If the Dow earns 10% per year over the next 20 years, the Dow will reach 88,000.

- If the Dow earns 12% per year over the next 20 years, the Dow will hit 117,000.

- If the Dow earns 15% per year over the next 20 years, the Dow will exceed 176,000.

Please note that I am not predicting that the Dow will produce such returns. I am merely showing you the mathematical results if such returns were to occur. Even a 3.5% average annual return would produce a 22,000 Dow!

So, I ask you: assuming you predicted any of these average annual returns (7%, 10%, 12%, 15%, or 3.5%), did you *also* predict the correct values that these returns would produce?

Probably not.

This demonstrates that you are willing to make predictions about the market without going to the trouble to *test your hypothesis*. Saying, "I think the market will gain 10%" without trying to determine what that statement means will cause you to make a bad decision. For no one ever gets excited when I offer them a 10% return—but everyone gets excited when I predict a 88,000 Dow. People guess that the Dow will make 25%—but they also predict that the future Dow will be 20,000. People who guess 5% think the future Dow will be 12,000.

---

[53] Indeed, if your answer was a positive number, this means you believe that stock prices will be higher in 20 years than they are today. Why, then, do you fear stocks?

And all of them worry that the current 9500 level is "too high."

If you think the market is "too high" you are looking at the past, not the future. Certainly, a 9,500 Dow seems high when you compare it to the 5,000 Dow of 1996 or the 3,000 Dow of 1990. But do you drive by looking in your rearview mirror?

Look where you're going, not where you've been. And look at the horizon, not the bumper in front of you.

Greed

Unfortunately, some people take the data offered above—a 155,000 Dow in 20 years!—and get far too excited. "Man, I can't wait to get in! Buy now!"

Greed—*overconfidence in the market*—is as dangerous to your financial health as fear.

Imagine that you've decided to buy a stock, which is priced at $20 per share. At what price per share will you sell?

In my seminars, 90% of the audience state a price of $30 or $40 a share. What I find astounding is that $24 represents a 20% gain. Yet, $24 doesn't sound like much, does it? People sit with bank CDs earning 4%, but they suddenly demand a 50% ($30) or 100% ($40) gain in their stocks. You greedy little pig. Remember that Wall Street saying: both bulls and bears make money, but pigs get slaughtered.

One more thing. Did you select a selling price that was below 20? In my seminars, virtually no one does. Thus, it never occurred to you that the stock might actually might go down in value!

I know what you're saying. "Why would I buy a stock that's going to go down?" Apparently, if my seminar experiences are of any value, it never occurs to people that stocks do this. Instead, people focus solely on how much money they want to earn. They almost never focus on how much money they're willing to lose, and it never occurs to them that a stock they buy might go down.

Thus, when market drops occur, you are shocked. Shock occurs when something unexpected happens. When you get shocked, your next reaction is: fear.

And we're right back where we started.

Optimism

Let's move on instead. Where greed means overconfidence in the market, *optimism means overconfidence in yourself.*

Thaler demonstrates optimism by asking his MBA students to anonymously write down where they expect to rank among the class. Of 125 students queried in 1998, 100% expected to finish in the top half of the class. Obviously, half were wrong. Kahneman found that most college students say they are less likely to die of cancer than their roommates. And most say they have a better sense of humor, too. Certainly, many are incorrect.

Overconfidence leads people to do dangerous things with their money. Because of your confidence, you're willing to take a huge risk with your money. You're willing to buy an investment based on your predictions of future interest rates, or currency fluctuations, or stock prices.

Unfortunately, your confidence is really overconfidence, and you're suffering from optimism. According to the academic data, optimists tend to:

- exaggerate their talents
- think they're better at investing than they really are
- often overestimate their knowledge
- exaggerate their ability to control events

and as a result of all this, they

- underestimate the risks they are taking

These traits were revealed in a study done by one of Kahneman's students, Terrence Odean. A guy who clearly needs a hobby, he examined hundreds of thousands of trades in 10,000 accounts at a major discount brokerage firm.[54] He discovered that when investors sold a stock and quickly bought another, the stocks they sold subsequently grew in value 3.4% more than the stocks they bought. After factoring in transaction expenses, investors lost about 5% through this activity. Clearly, these investors were overconfident about their ability to pick future winners; they would have been better off doing nothing.

I have seen similar attitudes among people seeking to hire my financial planning firm. Some of the statements I've heard include:

- "I have money to invest in stocks. I know that stocks are about to rise right now."

- "I work for a great company, and because I work there, I know exactly what's going on. Therefore, I put all of my 401(k) money into my company's stock."

- "One of my investments has done better [or worse] than others. Therefore, I want to move money from other investments into this one [or move this money into other ones]."

- "I heard on the news [enter fact here]. Therefore, [enter prediction here] is going to happen next, so I want to [enter transaction here]."

There's an old Wall Street saying: Never confuse genius with a bull market. Please avoid overconfidence, for it could ruin you.

---

[54] At discount brokerage firms, investors buy and sell on their own, without the advice or counsel of a broker.

Pessimism

Pessimism is a *lack of confidence in yourself*. And while many people reject the notion that they are an optimist, nearly everyone agrees they are a pessimist: they don't want to invest in stocks because they don't think they're good enough to pick the right stock.

Consider this question:

Do you have the ability to pick the best mutual funds?

You probably chuckled to yourself at this notion. *Of course not!*, you say. You know you're not good at picking investments (often a result of past experience) and therefore, you don't even want to try.

This is an excellent demonstration of pessimism, and this lack of confidence in your own abilities prevents you from investing. If this psychological phenomenon is legitimate—if indeed, you really are as bad at investing as you think you are— then you'd be correct to stay out of the markets. So let's examine the situation more closely.

We'll begin with a simple question:

Do you think you're able to pick the best mutual fund every year?

I'm certain you said no. With 10,000 mutual funds in the marketplace, you've got only a 0.0001% chance of picking the fund that's destined to become this year's "number one" fund. You know this is impossible, and this is why you don't even try.

The personal finance press plays on this emotion. By offering you "six sizzling stocks for the summertime," they make you believe that *they* know what the hot picks are, helping to reinforce your feelings of inadequacy because you can't do what they do. By predicting "winners" with every issue and every broadcast, they make you think that financial ruin awaits you if you fail to make the right picks. All this leads you to stay out of the market.

The most interesting part of this situation is that although pessimists are convinced that they are unable to pick the best fund, they fail to realize that they are equally unlikely to pick the worst fund. Even if they did, they'd have done fine, because the worst stock fund of the past 10 years made more money than the average CD rate. But this is something the personal finance press doesn't want you to know, because it diminishes your need to rely on them for "hot picks"—picks which are, by the way, consistently bad.

And the best point is this: even though the worst fund did better than CDs, you're not likely to pick it—any more than you're likely to pick the best. Instead, you're much more likely to pick the average fund—and the average fund is good enough for you to achieve financial success.

So, put aside your pessimism. Quit worrying that you're not going to pick the best fund. After all, this is not a horse race, and you don't have to pick the best horse. Rather, you're playing horseshoes, and being close is good enough to win. As Warren Buffet once said, "It's better to be approximately right than precisely wrong."

This leads us to something called . . .

Regret

Regret means *wishing you hadn't done something you've done*. Essentially, regret makes you feel stupid. Since none of us want to feel that way, we'll do almost anything to avoid regret. It's a powerful emotion, and the focus of much study in behavioral economics.

Thaler offers an example of the things people will do to avoid regret. Say you and your brother have the same financial circumstances, and the same attitude toward investing. Suddenly, your uncle dies. In his will, he leaves you with $10,000 in U.S. T-bills and he leaves your brother $10,000 in a risky high-tech stock. Neither of you are comfortable with these investments; the treasuries are too conservative for you, and the stock is too risky for your brother. What will you each do?

According to Thaler's research—which I can confirm through my experience in our financial planning firm—you are both highly likely to do *nothing at all*. The reason: you are afraid that selling what you've inherited might prove to be the wrong thing to do. Thaler believes that people fear doing a dumb thing more than they fear failing to do a smart thing. *I'd rather hold a safe Treasury than buy a stock that might lose money, you say. I'd better hold this risky stock in case it rises, rather than move to something safe*, your brother says. Sound familiar?[55]

Investors will do certifiably crazy things to avoid regret. They'll hold a stock that's fallen sharply in value—because people often feel that they haven't lost money if they haven't yet sold the stock. Selling would force them to admit failure—and that causes regret.

It is unfortunate when people allow their emotions to determine their actions, because the math tells us that the opposite action is best. Say you invested $1,000 into a stock which has suddenly fallen 50% to $500. You don't want to sell because doing so would force you to admit you failed— something optimists can't acknowledge about themselves. So you hold on, waiting for the investment to return to its original level. There are several problems with this strategy:

- A $500 investment must gain 100% to reach $1,000—even though the investment only lost 50%. Thus, it's twice as hard to grow as it is to fall.

- The investment might indeed grow 100%—but it could take much longer for this to happen than for an alternative investment to achieve this goal. Refusing to sell and move on could prove very costly in terms of future missed opportunities.

---

[55] In *The New Rules of Money* (which you've certainly gone out and bought by now), I offer another reason for an heir's unwillingness to sell. Rule 56 cautions that heirs tend to treat inherited stocks and funds as heirlooms, not as financial instruments.

- Your feelings that "there is no loss until I sell" is unshared by anyone else. Say a stranger offers to buy your car from you, and you agree on a price of $10,000. The stranger offers to pay you with shares of a stock that are currently worth $5,000. When you object, the stranger says, "But it was worth $10,000 when I bought the stock!" This makes no sense to anyone but the stranger.

Here's another example. You know that the best way to invest a lump sum is all at once, in a highly diversified fashion. But many people who suddenly have money to invest prefer to invest a small portion over long periods—to dollar-cost-average their way into the market. This is not the proper format for dollar cost averaging, and it results in poor investment performance, but people do it anyway. Why? Because they are afraid that if they invest all at once, the market might crash soon after. Thus, by dollar cost averaging, they are trying to avoid regret. As Kahneman has observed, such an action might help you protect yourself against regret, but it won't make you rich.

Hindsight

Hindsight—*the tendency to overemphasize the past*—is closely associated with regret. We look backward and wish we had done something different. Often, we chastise ourselves for the mistakes we made. Why did we do such a dumb thing? Why didn't we see that such-and-such was the right thing to do?

The reason you did what you did was that what you did was quite reasonable when you did it. Today, with the benefit of hindsight, we can see that it wasn't effective, but you couldn't possibly have known that then.

I recently took a call from a viewer of my TV show. He wanted to know if he should fire his financial advisor. He explained that his return for the past four years was 14%. Not bad, but certainly well below the average performance of the U.S. stock market.

"Well," I asked him, "Are you invested exclusively in U.S. stocks?" If he was, I'd agree that his advisor had given him underperforming stocks.

"No, I'm highly diversified," he replied. "I'm in bonds, and real estate, and internationals as well as stocks."

On that basis, I explained, I didn't see a problem. In the past four years, U.S. stocks outperformed all other asset classes. Thus, if he owned such a diversified portfolio, a 14% average return seemed quite reasonable—especially considering that some of the asset classes he owned had actually lost money over the past four years.

"But that's my concern," the caller said. "If my advisor had put all my money into stocks, I'd be much better off. Instead, he gave me a bunch of internationals that have stunk. I think I should fire him over that."

This caller failed to recognize that he was suffering from hindsight, and that this was the basis for his feelings of regret. Looking backward, it was easy to see that U.S. stocks would outperform foreign stocks, but you couldn't know that four years ago. Back then, allocating your assets among both asset classes was a prudent course of action. If the internationals had beaten the U.S., the caller would probably now be complaining about the poor performance of the U.S. stocks instead of the other way around. And if the advisor had recommended that his client place 100% of his money into U.S stocks—just one asset class, the client would have rejected the advice as too risky. But today, he complains that his advisor failed to do this.

What is most interesting is that the caller was completely unable to recall the events of four years ago that led him to follow the advisor's recommendations. This is not unusual. According to research done by Kahneman, most people cannot remember their prior predictions. And few are ever called on to do so.

For the guys who spill across CNBC every day, that's a critical point. Dozens of market analysts, economists, and money managers prance across the screen, each of them being asked by the host, "What's hot? What's going on? What do you like these days? Where are you putting your money?"

And as these guys rattle off their hot picks, you are impressed with their talent, their confidence, and their credibility. But there are two questions the hosts never ask them.

- What did you recommend the last time you were on the show?

- How did those recommendations work out?

People cannot remember their prior predictions. For proof, turn to politics, and answer this question:

Quick! Give me the name of a governor!

Did you name the governor of your own state? Or did you say *Jesse Ventura*? Many people who don't even know their own governor's name know his. You probably even know the state for which he's the governor![56]

Jesse Ventura won his election with 37% of the vote, but in a survey four months after the election, 80% of those surveyed said they voted for him. Were 43% deliberately lying? Or were they simply assuming, since their *optimism* led them to feel confident that they would have voted for the winner, that they must have voted for Jesse. You tell me.

Let's put this into the context of the stock market. From January 1, 1998, through July 17, 1998, the S&P 500 gained 16%. From July 17 to October 8, the market lost 19.2%—including a one-day drop in the Dow of 502 points, the worst since the Crash of 1987. From October 9 to the end of that year, the market gained 28.1%—recovering as quickly as it fell.

Today, many people believe the market's sudden decline and even more sudden recovery was obvious. Hindsight makes people think that, *I should've seen it coming*. It can lead to *over-confidence* because if you think you should have "seen it coming," you'll begin to think that you will be able to see the next one coming—and of course, you get just as blindsided.

---

[56] Minnesota.

If you're going to look backward, do so for the purpose of studying history, not to reevaluate why you did or didn't do something.

Quilting

The human psyche tends *to perceive trends where none exist.* In the world of investing, this is called the "hot hand fallacy." Here's an example.

Say we are about to study a group of eight money managers over a three-year period. One of them will produce the best three-year track record, another will produce the worst, and the rest will fall in between these extremes. Let's label these subjects as Managers A through H.

Let's say that, after year one, Managers E, F, G, and H make more money than Managers A, B, C, and D.

In year two, we discover that Managers G and H do better than E and F, and in year three, of the remaining two best managers to date, G makes more money than H. Therefore, G has been the only manager to produce an above-average performance in each of the three years. Clearly then, G is the best money manager.

And it's all random chance. After all, *somebody* will produce a three-year track record that is better than everybody else. But that doesn't mean it has anything to do with skill or talent. Mathematically speaking, somebody must be best.

But none of this matters to the personal finance press. They'll put Manager G on the cover of their magazine. He'll be interviewed on television, and quoted frequently in newspapers. His company will run a big ad campaign touting his fabulous performance, and investors will throw money at him. And later, when his "hot hand" cools, everyone will wonder what went wrong.

Of course, nothing will have "gone wrong." Since he did well merely by chance, he'll soon stop doing well—again, merely by chance. If you think I'm kidding, look at the baseball statistics assembled by Bruce Bemis, a mathematics professor at Westminster College. He showed that even in a league where everyone bats .250, at least one 20-game hitting streak can be expected to occur. Similar studies have shown that, despite the fact that a no-hitter is one of the most talked-about events in the game, no-hitters occur exactly as often as they are mathematically predicted to occur. Fans go nuts over them anyway.

Baseball isn't unique. Tversky, along with colleagues Gilovich and Vallone, showed in this 1985 basketball study that players are never "hot" or "cold"—despite what fans think. After analyzing the results of players' shots in hundreds of games, including normal play and free-throws, the only deviations from a player's normal performance that they could find were purely from random chance. Clearly, by labeling a player as "hot," fans are assigning to the player a pattern of unusual success that simply doesn't exist.

Data from the financial markets provide further evidence of this. If outperformance is due to skill, rather than chance, outperforming investments could be expected to continue to outperform.

But that doesn't happen. As I showed you in *The Truth About Money*[57]:

- In a five-year study of the SEI Equity Universe, 52% of the mutual funds that began the study in the top quartile finished the study in the bottom two quartiles. Likewise, of all the funds that started in last place, 50% finished in the top two quartiles.

- In a separate three-year study of all Morningstar five-star rated funds, 63% fell to below-average at the end of the study.

- A review of funds that were top-ranked by Lipper over five-year rolling periods showed that 42% of the top funds fell to the bottom two ranks in the following period, while 36% of the bottom-ranked funds later rose to the top two ranks.

---

[57] More plagiarism. But what the heck; *Truth* is a classic in the field of personal finance. At least, that's what my mother tells all her friends.

- Ten years after being named to the Forbes Honor Roll, funds that made the list earned an average of 24% less than the industry averages.

Clearly, just because a fund is ranked "best" does not mean it will continue to offer such stellar performance. Don't fall victim to quilting, for unlike your favorite quilt, investments offer no identifiable patterns.

Loss Aversion

This phenomenon tells us that *most people dislike losses more than they like gains.* Would you rather forgo a gain than incur a loss? Most people would.

Let's bet on a coin toss. If you lose the bet, you lose $100. How much money must you be able to win in order for you to consider this an acceptable bet?

Your answer: _____

The average answer, according to the experts, is $200–$250. If you said $200, this means you consider losses to be twice as bad as you consider winning to be good. When I conduct the experiment in seminars, there's always someone in the room who demands $1,000 as their prize. Such a person fears losses so badly that they insist on winning ten times as much in order to play the game.[58]

Let's try this coin toss again. This time, I will offer a different set of rules: If you win, you win $100, but if you lose, you will lose $200. Will you take this bet?

Your answer: _____

---

[58] If your answer was $100, congratulations. You responded rationally.

Of course, you said no. Nobody would take this bet. And yet, when we did this the first time, such a scenario is exactly what you demanded: you faced the possibility of losing $100, but you wanted the other guy to risk losing $200. Now, with the roles reversed, you refuse to participate. I hope you can see that you are being irrational about this!

And since you won't find anyone willing to take such a bet, you discover that you never play. I have had plenty of people tell me—with all sincerity—that they want an investment "that offers a 25% return with no risk." Of course, I am unable to give them such an investment. Result: their money sits in the bank for decades, earning 3% per year. One woman recently asked me how to start saving money. I suggested mutual funds. "But do I have to pay taxes on them?" she asked. When I replied that, yes, taxes would be owed on the profits, she told me she wasn't interested. Result: she doesn't accumulate any savings.

By irrationally making demands that no one can meet, you lose valuable opportunities to accumulate wealth. Be willing to accept losses. Only that way are you able to enjoy the gains you need to build wealth. And if you're uncertain as to how to build that wealth without sacrificing too much safety, return to our talk on diversification.

Accidental Anchoring

Accidental anchoring is *the mistake of assigning importance to random points*. When I asked you to consider whether the market is too high right now, there was an inherent assumption that the current market level matters in the decision-making process of whether to invest. And, as my example showed you, the current level doesn't matter.[59]

In my seminars on this subject, I ask the audience at the start of the session to pretend that they've just joined a company's 401(k) plan. They have already decided to

---

[59] What does matter is the rate of return you expect to earn in the future.

contribute money to the plan; all that's left for them to do is decide how they want to invest their contributions. I present them with four investment choices:

a) guaranteed fixed account

b) U.S. government securities fund

c) blue chip stock fund

d) aggressive growth fund

I tell the audience to allocate their contributions in any manner they wish, so that the total equals 100%. I offer no help or guidance in this decision. Later in the session, we repeat this exercise. But this time, I offer the audience a 401(k) plan that offers 10 choices instead of four. They are:

a) guaranteed fixed account

b) U.S. government securities fund

c) high yield bond fund

d) blue chip stock fund

e) growth fund

f) S&P 500 Index fund

g) aggressive growth fund

h) small cap fund

i) emerging markets fund

j) international stock fund

When they're done, I ask them to tally the total percentage that they had allocated to choices D through J. This represents the total that they have allocated to stocks. I then ask them to return to the first example, and see how much they allocated there to choices C & D.

Almost without exception, my seminar participants discover that the amount of money they've placed into stocks in the first exercise was not the same as the amount they chose to contribute to stocks in the second exercise.

But why not? Seemingly, nothing has changed. The client isn't different. His or her circumstances and goals are not different. Why, then, did they create two different allocation models?

The answer lies in accidental anchoring. Rather than approaching the decision with a prior determination of how much of your retirement account you want invested into stocks, you acted passively, reacting to the choices made available to you by your employer. In the first test, 50% of the plan's choices were stocks, while 70% of choices were stocks in the second exercise. This causes almost everyone to make different allocation decisions. And when employees know little about investing, they merely invest their money in equal amounts across all of the investment options available. That's fine—if the boss offers nothing but good choices. But if the plan is skewed toward one type of investment or another, employee contributions get equally skewed.

This has been proven in studies of major retirement plans. According to *Fortune* magazine, when TWA pilots were offered five stock funds and one income fund in their retirement plan, 75% of the money went into stocks. But when the University of California offered one stock fund and four fixed-income funds, only 34% of the money went into stocks. And look at the federal Thrift Savings Plan for government workers. Of its three choices, only one of them is stocks. So, it's no surprise that only 54% of the plan's assets are in stocks.

Do you think that relying on your employer's choices is too logical to be the wrong thing to do? That it doesn't demonstrate accidental anchoring well enough? Then consider this wild example, created by Professor Thaler. He had his students write down a totally arbitrary date in history by adding 400 to the last three digits of their Social Security Number. He then asked them to guess the year in which Attila the Hun invaded France.

Apparently, everyone relied on their random anchors to help them arrive at an answer, because the students who had low anchors were off by an average of only 175 years, while those who had high anchors were off by more than 500 years. Clearly, their starting point affected their estimates—even though their starting points were both random and completely irrelevant!

Here's another example: Let's say you're about to invest in one of seven telecommunications stocks. But which one?

I'm talking about the seven original Baby Bells, and studies show that when an investor owns just one of them, it's almost always their local phone company. New Yorkers love Nynex, while Chicagoland favors Ameritech. Clearly, each investor is attempting to choose the "best" stock. But if everyone is choosing their hometown favorite, six out of seven investors must be wrong. Clearly, they are allowing location to serve as an accidental anchor.

The next time you're faced with a decision, ask yourself if the parameters are valid, and why you're framing the decision within the context that you are. By paying attention, you'll be able to ditch that anchor before it sinks you.

Farming versus Foresting

Farming vs. Foresting is the *failure to focus on the entire scenario simultaneously.* Farmers, as you know, plant crops, one at a time. By contrast, forest rangers view the entire landscape at once. You must act like rangers, not farmers, if you are to succeed financially.

To demonstrate this, Dr. Kahneman and his colleague Mark Riepe offered a test that appeared in the *Journal of Portfolio Management.* It follows below. See how you do.

Below are two separate questions. Examine both before you answer either one.

Choose between:

A. a sure gain of $2,400

B. a 25% chance of making $10,000 and a 75% chance of gaining nothing.

Your answer: _____

Choose between:

C. a sure loss of $7,500

D. a 75% chance of losing $10,000 and a 25% chance of losing nothing.

Your answer: _____

Did you choose A and D? Just about everyone does. Next, consider this final question:

Choose between:

E. a 25% chance to win $2,400 and 75% chance to lose $7,600

F. a 25% chance to win $2,500 and 75% chance to lose $7,500

Your answer: _____

Did you choose F? Everybody does. But here's the interesting part: You rejected E even though E is the equivalent of A & D.

If you had properly considered the first two questions concurrently—as I told you to—you would have discovered this. And yet, even with my prompting, you failed to approach the quiz correctly. Imagine the quality of the financial decisions you make when you get no such prompting!

There are dozens of examples in personal finance where people make similar mistakes. It's called compartmentalizing, and we've already talked about it in this book. If you make a series of financial decisions one-at-a-time, each decision might seem to be the right one, yet you end up with two bad decisions instead of one good one—leaving you wondering why you haven't achieved financial success.

Do you compartmentalize? Sure you do: Suppose you go on vacation, taking along $500 as spending money. When you return home, you discover that you have $100 left over. Will you return that money to the investment or savings account it came from, or will you regard that $100 as "found money" and spend it?

Rational investors realize that *all* the money they have came from the same source—their hard work—and they treat all their money with equal sobriety. But those who compartmentalize treat this $100 as "money I intended to spend anyway" and since they haven't yet spent it, they feel free to do so. Result: these people have $100 less in savings than rational investors.

Don't be too quick to dismiss this psychological failing just because you think you wouldn't have spent that hundred bucks. In the real world, most incidents of compartmentalizing are much more complex. Some examples:

- you're carrying a credit card balance while also saving money for your kid's college tuition.

- You want to maximize your tax deductions but have a 15-year mortgage instead of a 30-year loan.

- You agree with the need to diversify your portfolio, but most of your money is invested in company stock anyway.

- You make extra principal payments to get your house paid off sooner while also saying that you are aren't saving enough for retirement.

In each of these scenarios, the two actions contradict each other, effectively reducing (and sometimes, preventing) your ability to achieve wealth. Yet I come across consumers who make this type of mistake all the time. Some of the more common examples:

- You open a mutual fund or brokerage account because you want to invest some money, but you give little thought to how that account should be registered (your name only? Joint with your spouse? Tenants by the Entirety or JTWROS? How about a custodial account in the name of your child? Or maybe a trust account?)

- You want to refinance to get a lower interest rate, but when examining the available interest rates offered by various loan programs, you fail to consider the cash flow requirements, lost investment opportunities, and resulting tax implications that will occur by choosing one loan over another.

- At work, you are given life insurance as an employee benefit. You name your spouse as beneficiary and children as secondary beneficiaries without regard to the fact that minor children are legally prohibited from owning assets.

It's understandable why people make these mistakes. Every economic decision you make has financial, tax, and legal ramifications—but you don't know about them and, too often, the people you're dealing with in each situation don't know, either. An insurance agent can tell you about the policy he's selling, but does he know about the policy's tax and estate implications? Stockbrokers know about their investments, but can they advise you on the tax implications of selling a stock or on the legal issues surrounding the account's registration? Your human resources officer at work can explain the benefits, but he or she knows nothing of your personal circumstances and is prohibited from giving advice. The accountant preparing your tax return can tell you to open an IRA for tax-savings, but is he or she qualified to offer investment advice? Your real estate agent wants to sell you a house, the mortgage broker wants you to get that loan, and the car dealer wants you to buy that auto, but what impact might each decision have on the rest of your personal finances?

Be aware of Farming vs. Foresting. In today's highly complex world of money, it's best to consult with skilled financial, tax, and legal advisors *before* you make any economic decision.

Summary

What happens when investors act out of fear or greed, display optimism or pessimism, fall victim to regret and hindsight, seek patterns where none exist, go to extreme lengths to avoid losses, tie themselves to faulty anchors, or farm instead of forest? Kahneman says it best:

> "Investors who are prone to these biases will take risks that they do not acknowledge, experience outcomes they did not anticipate, will be prone to unjustified trading, and may end up blaming themselves or others when the outcomes are bad."

Yeech.
Do yourself a favor. Avoid these mental missteps.

SECRET #5

They Don't Measure Their Success Against the Dow or the S&P 500.

SECRET #5
They Don't Measure Their Success Against the Dow or the S&P 500.

I am astounded at how often people focus on issues that are completely irrelevant to their financial success. For example, consider the performance of the S&P 500 Stock Index. Over the past five years, most stock mutual funds have failed to gain as much as the S&P. You've heard people say this many times, but what you do not realize is that this little factoid is pointless, and has little meaning for your life. Nevertheless, the statement has managed to garner incredible media attention—so much so that people who know nothing about investments are able to tell you that "mutual funds can't beat the S&P 500."

Of course, that assertion is wrong, as I explained thoroughly in *The New Rules of Money*[60]. But more important for us here is the fact that this statement is, for the millions of Americans trying to reach their financial goals, completely irrelevant.

It does not matter how the S&P 500 performs—or any other index, for that matter—unless your investments happen to consist of exactly that investment. And since your investments don't mimic the S&P (fortunately)[61], your investments can't be expected to perform identically.

In fact, I'm not even sure why the S&P is getting so much attention. It might have to with the fact that the standard-bearer for the market, the Dow Jones Industrial Average, consists of only 30 stocks—30 of the largest companies in the U.S. That's hardly a true representation of Corporate America.

---

[60] A not-so-subtle hint that you need to go read—or rather, buy—that book. Try amazon.com or barnesandnoble.com

[61] As *NRM* predicted, those who own S&P 500 index funds will regret it.

So the S&P 500—which tracks 500 stocks rather than 30—is a better gauge. But is it better than, say, the Wilshire 5000 which tracks (despite its name) all 7,200 of the country's listed stocks? And what about the Nasdaq, or EAFE indexes? They're valid, too. And they're not alone. In truth, indexes are everywhere. Dow Jones & Company alone offers 1,600 of them and many other competitors offer thousands more as well.[62]

All these indexes exist because companies make money selling their research to stock analysts, money managers, economists, government agencies, and think tanks. Standard and Poor's has done a particularly brilliant marketing job; by licensing its 500 Index to the mutual fund industry, it permitted the creation of mutual funds based on the index's makeup. (Until recently, Dow Jones & Company refused to license its Industrial Average index, which explains why there weren't any mutual funds that replicated the Dow.) Thus, more attention is paid to the S&P, in part, because if investors own an index fund, chances are it's an S&P 500 Index Fund.

But, as I've said, unless you own this index—and nothing but this index—how it's performing is irrelevant to your life. What matters instead is that the performance of your investments are matching the Individual Investor Index (I³).

You own this index, by the way. Everyone does. But not everyone knows they own it, or knows what their index is. If you hired a financial advisor, as my clients have done, the planner told you how much money your investments needed to earn each year, on average, for you to achieve your long-term financial objectives. In our firm, for example, our clients typically need to earn an average annual total return of 8% to 12%. Of course, in some years, they'll earn 20%, while in other years, they'll earn 3% or perhaps even lose a little money. But on average, 8% to 12% is the goal.

---

[62] Heck, even *I've* got a bunch of indexes. One, for example, is Ric Edelman's Valentine's Index, which tracks what it costs you to show your love every Feb. 14th. 1999's cost: $2,320.50.

Say a married couple, both 42, hires us for financial planning. They tell us they want to retire when they reach age 60, at which point they want an annual retirement income of $80,000. We analyze their situation and determine, based on their assets, pension, and social security projections, presumed inflation rates and life expectancies and so forth, as well as their continued ability to save monthly over the next 18 years, that they will be able to achieve their goals if their current investments produce an average annual total return of, say, 11%. This figure, then, becomes their Individual Investor Index. Thus, we'll recommend a basket of investments—called a portfolio—that, taken together, is designed to give the client the opportunity to earn, on average and over long periods, an annualized total return of 11%.

Now let's say that this client earns 14% in a given year, a year in which the S&P 500 produces 25%. Should the client be upset? Concerned?

How about *happy*? For that, indeed, is the attitude of the clients of our firm. They know their investments are not modeled after the S&P, so they're not tracking its performance. Nor are they comparing their own investment results to the S&P—or any other index, for that matter. Instead, they're doing what they should be doing: tracking their personal investment results to their own I³. And they realize that failure to meet their index in any one year is not necessarily a problem, although sustained underperformance over several years might be.[63]

And thus, you see why our clients are not concerned with the S&P. Instead of focusing their attention on statistics arbitrarily assembled by industry observers, they focus their attention on their own personal goals. If their goals are properly set, and if they are meeting their goals, then they're happy. As they should be.

---

[63] And then again, it might not. An I³ that called for an 11% average return might have based that projection on an assumed 4% inflation rate. If inflation is only 2%, a 9% return is just as effective in real economic terms, because the client still enjoyed a 7% after-inflation return.

Indeed, of our survey's respondents, only 15% compare their investments to the Dow and even fewer—11%—make comparisons to the S&P 500. And few of our clients even *know* whether their investments are outperforming these indexes. For the overwhelming majority, the indexes don't matter, because they know that the indexes have little relevance to their situation and goals.

What, then, does matter? The most common way our clients evaluate their overall portfolio is by examining *the percentage gain for the year*. Exactly as I described it above. They don't care what some external, arbitrary standard is doing. Instead, 85% of our clients are totally focused on their own situation. They know what their investments need to produce in order for them to achieve their goals, and therefore, those are the numbers they watch.

Some people, though, insist on comparing their investment performance to the S&P (or some other yardstick). Some of these folks have a diversified portfolio; others do not. Either way, they lose. Here's why: Those who *do not* have a diversified portfolio own nothing but stock funds, which they compare to the Dow or S&P. In making these comparisons, they'll discover that some of their investments will have beaten the indexes, while others did not. Discovering that some of their funds failed to beat the Dow or S&P will make them frustrated over what they perceive to be "lost opportunities." This emotional reaction will cause them to sell their losers in a futile attempt to invest in future winners and such market-timing activity will simply leave them equally frustrated next year when the process repeats itself.

Those who *do* have a diversified portfolio, meanwhile, are not solely invested in stocks, but they compare their portfolio to these indexes as though they were. Naturally, they are disappointed to discover that their more conservative approach didn't match the returns of the stock market, so they sell their non-stock holdings and move those assets into stocks, where they hope to gain the higher returns they've been missing. Like those above, these investors are also acting emotionally, and they are certain to be emotionally—and financially—dismayed when the stock market falls in value.

Successful investors avoid both of these traps. Because they understand what they own and why they own it, they evaluate their overall portfolio's results over long periods based on their own goals and objectives. They ignore media reports of "average market results," and if you want to become financially successful, you'll do the same.

SUCCESSFUL INVESTORS:
THEY DON'T MEASURE THEIR SUCCESS AGAINST THE DOW OR THE S&P 500.
"IN THEIR OWN WORDS"

I don't pay attention to the Dow or the S&P 500 because we own mutual funds.

My problem is that I get nervous when dealing with money—I'm from the old school of money where you save your money under a mattress—because I'm afraid that the money won't be there when the time comes to retire. I don't like risk. And I know I'll drive myself crazy if I look at the Dow and the S&P 500 day to day. I'm in it for the long haul, so I only look periodically because I know I'm not going to do anything about it.

I measure the progress of my investments by the annual statement I get. It gives me an overall picture of what my portfolio is doing. I take no action if one annual statement doesn't perform well because I'm in for the long term, not the short term.

Andy Taylor, retired officer, United States Marines. Currently an 8th grade social studies teacher. Raised in Camden and Margate, New Jersey

Phyllis Taylor, registered nurse, retired. Raised in Trenton, New Jersey

---

I kind of listen to what's going on with the Dow and the S&P, but I don't panic one way or another. It's so volatile.

I don't really think my success depends on what the Dow or

S&P are doing because the bulk of my money is invested for the long term and I'm not planning to use it for a while.

I don't try to measure the progress of my investments too closely. I get a statement every month and I look at it and just wait for the next one. If I had concerns, I'd call my investment advisor and see what is going on, but I haven't had to do that.

I'd tell investors who are trying to track their investments to "cool it." I believe you should be in the market for years; don't pay attention to the daily, weekly, or monthly fluctuations in the market.

Irene Henry, corporate secretary. Born in Czechoslovakia and raised in Belcamp, Maryland

---

§§

I've never paid attention to the Dow or the S&P 500. I've never bothered to learn about them and I don't care—they are the least of my worries.

At age 50, I had to walk out of a marriage—for peace, I needed to restart my life and get along by myself. My lawyer got me enough to buy a $10,000 car plus $25,000 (which wasn't much considering we owned a ranch and three drug stores; however, if I'd stayed with him I'd never be where I am today.)

I am from the early era, where men handled money and women kept their mouths shut. So, after receiving the $25,000 I needed to figure out what to do with it. It so happened that I ended up getting snowed in, in Denver, Colorado, where I spent four days visiting various investment companies. Finally, I found an investment advisor I felt I could work with. He asked me, "What do you want to do with your life?" I told him that I would love to go back to college. He told me to do it. So I did, and while I was in college, my money more than doubled.

It was during this time that I learned I could pay my own way and take care of myself. When I started earning money for myself, I suddenly realized I had been supporting my family on the ranch and the drug stores all along, but since I hadn't seen the money before, I wasn't aware of it. I have very few wants— I love the outdoors, live frugally, am not wasteful, pay cash for everything. I received my Ph.D. and am totally debt free.

When I was young and raising my family, my husband gave me a cash allowance of $15/person per week. This meant that my children and I had to learn to grow our own vegetables, can foods, make our own clothes, furniture, drapes, etc . . . Any paychecks I received went straight into one bank account that my husband controlled. Even though I managed the drug stores, he handled the cash. I think the reason I've been able to save so much is because I left my husband, put my faith in a financial advisor, and to this day, I have never touched the original $25,000 that I got from the divorce. Instead, I have kept getting good advice and adding to it. And I've never looked at the Dow or the S&P the entire time.

I'd tell people to forget about the indexes. Get good advice instead. Security is a state of mind. People don't really need to make a lot of money to be successful. Invest for the long term and ride the waves.

Name withheld, senior program scientist and author

I don't think it's important to pay attention to the Dow or the S&P 500. I'm a long-term investor. My investment success does not depend on what the Dow or the S&P 500 is doing. My investments are diversified and balanced enough that the Dow won't make a difference. In my opinion, if people feel they need to follow the Dow, they are investing the wrong way.

Jack McGaughy, computer analyst, retired. Wyomissing, Pennsylvania

Loy McGaughy, desktop publisher. Raised in Riverside, California

I don't watch the news reports about the Dow or the S&P because they don't have a direct effect on us—we own mutual funds. We're fairly diversified and our strategy is not just based on what the stock market is doing. For those who feel intimidated, I'd say you shouldn't be watching the stock market every day. You need to be more concerned about your own personal strategy and investment diversification.

I don't feel it's important to be able to talk about the Dow, nor do I feel that the Dow has much impact on my ability to invest successfully. Instead, I measure the success of our investments by looking at the total value of our investments, and to see whether they are achieving the goals we have set. I'd advise others to do the same.

Instead of watching the Dow, I'd tell others to be consistent about committing yourself to investing on a regular basis, regardless of how much or how little money you have. Pay yourself first.

Rosemarie Assad, biochemist and homemaker. Raised in Moorestown, New Jersey

Daniel Abe Assad, periodontist. Raised in Donora, Pennsylvania

---

I see the news reports about the Dow and S&P 500, but I don't react, because I know that my investment success doesn't depend on what those stock indexes are doing.

I don't measure my investments right now, and I don't know if I'll ever need to measure it. Doing so leads to impulse buying and selling.

Robert L. Adams, retired Army Officer and retired human resources manager. Raised in Joplin, Missouri and other places as an "Army brat"

Lucile Overton Adams, housewife and receptionist / secretary. Raised in Newport News, Virginia

Although I pay attention to the Dow and the S&P, they are just indicators. You don't really need to know about them or understand them to invest successfully.

Owen Allen, association executive, retired. Raised in Trinidad, Colorado

Nina May Allen, school librarian, retired. Raised in Cody, Wyoming

---

To those that feel intimidated about the Dow, I'd say: I understand. I'm not interested, either. I think it's boring! Don't worry about it!

We measure the progress of our investments by tracking our investments ourselves. We are paying for advice on our investments and we keep an eye on it to be sure our advisor is doing a good job.

Karen Bretthauer, systems accountant for the Department of Agriculture. Raised in Albany, New York

---

I was one of those people who felt intimidated by the Dow—before, I avoided it. I think it's important to be able to somewhat understand the Dow and the S&P 500, but we look at our monthly and quarterly statements to measure our success, as opposed to following the Dow or the S&P 500. The Dow is not central to our focus.

Name withheld, IBM retiree. Raised in Rochester, New Jersey

We pay attention to the Dow and the S&P 500 only a little bit. How can you not? It's always quoted by the press. We don't know exactly what the Dow and the S&P 500 represent, but you always hear about it when it goes down. I'd tell people not to feel intimidated by the Dow, just take time to consult with a financial planner, and do some reading on your own in newspapers and magazines.

No, I don't think it's important to be able to talk extensively about the Dow or the S&P 500. I don't think as lay people we need to know all the technical terms and ins and outs of the Dow or the S&P 500. If you have a resource center for financial information, use it. Our ability to invest successfully depends on our own decision making—and our ability to gain knowledge doesn't depend on the Dow or the S&P 500 but on seeking the best advice we can.

If I could go backwards in time . . . I wish that we had gotten a financial advisor sooner than we did. We didn't look at our investment statements thoroughly. My husband is a conservative investor, and for a long time his 401(k) money didn't earn what it could have.

The day you start working, start investing for your retirement, look at it as long-term, and spend the money for a competent financial advisor. I'm talking early . . . my son is a teenager and he's starting to invest for retirement now.

Susan M. Fake, bookkeeper. Raised in Rochester, New York

Barry H. Fake, self-employed paint contractor. Raised in Reading, Pennsylvania

SECRET #6

They Devote Less than Three Hours Per Month to Their Personal Finances.

And That Includes the Time They Spend Paying Bills. And Budgeting? They Never Bothered.

SECRET #6

They Devote Less than Three Hours Per Month to Their Personal Finances.

And That Includes the Time They Spend Paying Bills. And Budgeting? They Never Bothered.

If my clients' experiences and habits are any guide, there seems to be a direct correlation between the amount of time you spend on your personal finances and your overall financial success. And the correlation is this: the more time you spend dealing with money matters, the less successful you are.

It's another powerful example of the counterintuitive nature of money. Many people think that those who accumulate wealth devote substantial amounts of time and energy to do so. And they excuse away their own financial failure to their own inability (or, sometimes, unwillingness) to focus on finances. I'd love to track the market during the day, they'll tell you, but I'm tied up at work, or busy raising my family. I already work two jobs, some will say pejoratively, and I don't need or want another. But like all other excuses, these are merely that: excuses. You can offer whatever reasons you like for why you don't have more money than you do, and the results will be the same: you'll be as poor in the future as you are today.

So let me tip over the pedestal on which many stand to proclaim why they have no wealth. "I don't have the time to devote attention to my finances!" they say. Well, if my clients are any guide, time is perhaps the one thing that's not a prerequisite for achieving wealth.[64] Indeed, according to the

---

[64] Lest anyone misunderstand me, I'm referring here to "time devoted to finances" not to the "length of time you let your money grow."

findings of our research, our clients spend on average 2.4 hours per month on money matters. And that includes the time they devote to paying their bills.

This will shock many people. After all, I know of many folks who spend hours upon hours just balancing—or rather, juggling—their checkbook. And yet, from my years serving as an advisor to thousands of consumers, I can tell you that there are certain traits common to American consumers, including:

1) The less money you have, the more checking and savings accounts you have.

2) The less money you have, the more time you spend paying your bills.

3) The less money you have, the more you micromanage it.

4) The less money you have, the more you act like you have a lot of it.

Let me elaborate on these traits for you.

According to my research, 82% of financially successful people have two checking accounts and one savings account. But people who earn less money, and who have little money, often have three or even five bank accounts—and they're constantly transferring money between them in an endless game of shuffleboard. She's got one account into which she deposits her salary; he's got one, too. They have a third account, jointly held, to which they each contribute a portion of their salaries for the purpose of paying household bills. They have a fourth account for savings (though money rarely gets deposited there, and what little money is there is usually withdrawn or transferred to other accounts to pay bills). And there's often a fifth account that exists largely because the bank is (or was) more convenient than the others, or because it offers higher interest rates, lower fees, or some other attraction.

Many people waste many hours each month in pointless efforts to maintain these accounts, insure they have sufficient balances, and reconcile the statements. As my clients demonstrate, your life can be much simpler by reducing the number of bank accounts you have.

But I can't do that! you say. *How will I be able to track where the money came from?*

You already know where your money comes from. You don't need multiple bank accounts to help you figure that out.

But what about tracking where my money is going? Without separate accounts, I won't be able to keep track of everything!

Nonsense. Although tracking expenses is an important task for those who are trying to minimize frivolous expenses, you don't need multiple bank accounts to help you do it. In fact, the more accounts you have, the harder and more time consuming it is to track your expenses. Today, many banks offer online services that automatically track your expenses for you, and software programs such as Quicken also enable you to do this—they even accept downloads from your bank so you can avoid re-typing the data into your home computer.

And you don't even need a computer to track expenses. Chapter 51 of *The Truth About Money*[65] shows you how to do it with just pen and paper. So if you want to track your expenses, you can do it either with or without a computer. But either way, only one bank account is required.

The irony is that many people who are failing financially feel in control of their finances solely because they devote meticulous attention to their bank accounts. A great example of this was Mike and Sally. They were introduced to me by a local television news reporter, who asked me to counsel several couples for a series the station was doing on personal finance. The news station invited viewers to send a letter if they were interested in being part of the series. The show's producers

---

[65] Good news: you don't have to buy a computer. But you do have to go buy my first book. Heh heh heh.

selected five. My assignment was to meet with the five and give each a financial plan. In exchange for getting my help for free, the couple agreed to be profiled on TV.

One couple stands out. Mike was 35, a mechanic earning $45,000. Sally was 34, a stay-at-home mom raising their eight-year-old son, Shawn. They had $18,000 scattered among four bank accounts. Their bills were typical: One mortgage, two car payments, and the usual expenses for food and clothes and such. They owed $4,000 to credit cards. Although his employer offered a 401(k) plan, Mike wasn't participating, and neither of them had an IRA. They had no life insurance, no disability insurance, and no wills. Investments? None. No stocks. No bonds. No mutual funds. And no money set aside for Shawn's college or their own retirement.

But her checkbooks were immaculate.

Sally maintained extraordinarily detailed records of every expenditure. Mike's paycheck went into one bank account. From there, she would write checks payable to other accounts, two of which were at different institutions. One of these was for the monthly mortgage and car payments. Another was for routine bills; the fourth was what she called a "rainy day" fund (and what I call a slush fund) she'd make payments to it if she had the cash, and she wrote checks from it if she lacked money in other accounts.

As any corporate comptroller can tell you, handling multiple cash management accounts is hard work. And Sally lives to prove it. She pays all bills within 24 hours of receipt, then carefully records each transaction in a separate notebook. Entries are color-coded: I saw entries variously marked in green, blue, red, yellow, purple, and black, and although Sally explained her system to me, I can't remember which color signified what. She could have sent Shawn to college on what she spent on markers alone.

Sally also maintained separate file folders to safeguard the bills. Before filing them away, she'd record the expenses in her journal, then note on each bill the date it was paid and the check number. The fact that this information appears on her monthly statement didn't seem to matter. The folders were then stored, alphabetically, in a desk drawer.

Sally brought all her files, journals, and checkbooks to our first meeting, as I had requested. Actually, as I do for all first appointments, I had requested that they bring *all* their financial papers: bank, brokerage, and investment account statements, employee benefits information, tax returns, wills and trust documents, insurance policies, and data pertaining to any real estate they owned. The only documents they brought were Sally's banking materials.

She was darn proud of it. And rightly so. By her own estimate, Sally spends 10–15 hours *per week* managing her household's finances. Not a penny comes in or goes out without her approval. Did Shawn get an allowance? No, but Mike did. And if he needed more cash, he had to talk with Sally first. Sally knew that most of her friends—and both of their families—didn't manage money well. But Sally and Mike knew exactly where their money was going.

Unfortunately, Sally and Mike think *managing the household's personal finances* means *just paying the bills*. It doesn't. So although Sally was spending huge amounts of time paying the bills—equivalent to a part-time job—she and Mike were ignoring all other aspects of personal finance.

As you might expect, I recommended that:

1) They both get wills, naming a guardian to raise their son in the event they both die.

2) He needed to buy life insurance, since he's the sole wage earner, to protect her and their son in case he dies.

3) She needed to buy life insurance, so he could afford to pay for help in caring for their son in case she dies.

4) He needed to buy disability income insurance, in case an injury or illness prevents him from working.

5) He needed to join his 401(k) plan at work, funding it to the maximum he's permitted.

6) Both he and she should open IRAs accounts and contribute $2,000 each to the plan every year.

7) They should pay off their credit card debts and transfer some of their remaining savings and into mutual funds.

8) They begin a formal savings plan to set aside money regularly for their son's college and their own retirement.

9) They eliminate three of the four bank accounts, which are redundant and serve little purpose other than to increase Sally's workload.

Of my nine recommendations:

1) They decided not to get the wills, since they "don't have enough money to worry about."

2) They decided not to buy life insurance on him because he's got coverage from his job, equal to his annual salary. They chose to ignore what she would do for money in the second year following Mike's death, nor did they explain what they would do if Mike quit or was fired from his job (either of which would cause him to lose his coverage).

3) They decided not to buy life insurance on her. No reasons were offered.

4) They decided not to buy disability insurance on him, because it was too expensive.

5) They decided not to join the 401(k), because they couldn't afford the cut in pay required to do so.

6) They decided not to open IRA accounts. No reason was given.

7) They chose not to pay off the credit cards, arguing that they didn't have enough money to do so, and they

decided not to buy mutual funds, expressing concern that mutual funds can lose money.

8) They decided not to establish a formal savings plan. They felt this was unnecessary since they were already saving money through Sally's bill-paying efforts. When I informed them that their efforts over the past 13 years had resulted in net accumulated savings of $14,000—enough to produce a monthly income at retirement of roughly $95 per month—they were unmoved.

9) They decided, well, I think you know what they decided.

For a long time, my colleagues and I tried to figure out why the couple rejected all my ideas. After all, they *volunteered* to receive a financial plan; it wasn't solicited. We came up with several possibilities for their inaction, including:

1) The recommendations were terrible. (Not a chance!)[66]

2) The advice was free. Had they paid for it, like typical clients, they would have had greater inclination and incentive to act on the information. (I don't think this is the reason. They traveled quite a distance to visit with me—twice—and were interviewed for two hours by the TV News crew at their home. They also had to complete a homework assignment I gave them. Even though they didn't spend money to get their plan, they invested a considerable amount of time.)

3) They signed up just because they wanted to be on TV. (Nah. This couple was very friendly and down-to-earth—yet private and quiet. They weren't Jerry Springer guest types seeking 15 minutes of fame.)

---

[66] Awright, who's the wise guy who said that?!

4) They didn't act on the plan because they never wanted
    one. Instead, Sally simply wanted to show us what a
    good job she was doing at paying the bills.

I hope that doesn't sound too harsh. Let me explain. We
encourage people to get a review of their finances, for getting a
second opinion can be helpful. Some of the people who accept
our offer truly need our help, and they're grateful to get it.
Others need mere tweaking—they just need to consider making
subtle (and occasionally not terribly important) changes in the
way they're handling their finances. A few we slap on the back
and say, "Just keep on doing what you're doing!"

But sometimes, we come upon people who are failing at
most elements of personal finance, but they are managing to do
one or two things really well. Inevitably, those are the only
things they want to talk about. They don't want to discuss their
weaknesses or listen to any advice we might offer. To put it
quite bluntly, these people just want to brag.

Look at my stock portfolio! they say. But what about your
mortgage, taxes, wills, and insurance, we reply. Never mind
that, they say. *Look at my stock portfolio!*

It's not uncommon for my colleagues and me to see this.

But financially successful Americans don't commit this
error. They don't focus on any one part of their finances to the
exclusion of all others. They don't have four bank accounts
while lacking investments. They don't devote hours to bill
paying while ignoring insurance. And instead of counting their
chickens, they're busy trying to produce more eggs.

Perhaps the most remarkable thing about wealthy
Americans is that they have been able to handle all aspects of
their personal finances without treating the subject as a second
job. After all, Sally might have avoided insurance and investments simply because she feared the time it would take. I mean,
if she's spending 15 hours a week just paying the bills, imagine
the time she'd spend if she added these other tasks to her list!

But none of that is necessary. Although it's true that many
people do indeed devote 10–20 hours or more per week to their
finances, these people are hobbyists, and they'd rather play with

their money than join a bowling league. But you do not need to enjoy dealing with money in order to succeed at it—anymore than you must enjoy brushing your teeth to avoid cavities. And you certainly are not required to spend multiple hours per week. After all, none of my firm's clients do.

According to my study:

- 85% of my firm's clients spend *less than three hours per month* paying their bills. More than a third do it in under an hour.

- A whopping 97% devote *less than two hours per month* to balancing their checkbook—and 9% don't even bother to balance it at all!

- And 82% devote *less than three hours per month* to their investments. Only 5% spend more than five hours per month.

And there's even more good news for you. My clients consider budgeting to be a complete waste of time, evidenced by the fact that only 6% have and follow a budget. And don't think that this is only because my clients are rich, and that rich people don't need to follow a budget, because only 21% of my clients say that they *ever* had a budget—and even when they had it, only 24% strictly followed it. So if you've been struggling with a budget, and feeling guilty for not following it closely, you can stop—both the budgeting and feeling guilty!

On the other hand, there's widespread agreement that tracking expenses is worthwhile, because 76% of my clients say they do it. This is an important distinction, because there's a big difference between *budgeting* and *tracking expenses*. The former is a promise of how you *will* spend money; the latter reflects how you actually *do* spend it. And while budgeteers often spend more than they had earlier promised themselves—creating such problems as falling into debt—trackers keep themselves, well, on track toward their goals. You should do the same.

So if you've claimed that the reason you aren't rich is because you don't have time to devote to your personal finances, you need to find another excuse. Because as my clients show, accumulating wealth takes very little time out of your day.

Successful Investors:
They Devote Less than Three Hours Per Month to Their Personal Finances.
And That Includes the Time They Spend Paying Bills.
And Budgeting? They Never Bothered.

" In Their Own Words "

I use Quicken, which helps me keep track of what's coming in and going out. It takes me about 2–3 hours per month. We have two checking accounts, one is for major items, like taxes. We used to have three, but we realized we don't need the third account.

We don't use a budget, but we do understand how much we need to pay the bills. We always keep cash on hand for emergencies.

Name withheld, transcriber of medical records

Spouse, former owner of service station

My sister and I live together. We have one bank account that we use to pay all the bills. We both used to have checking accounts, but now that my sister is retired, we use one joint account. It takes about two hours for her to pay the bills, which is fine, because I hate doing it!

It's important to be aware of your income vs. your expenses. You shouldn't spend what you don't have—but too many people do. In fact, this country has gone wacko! Too many people spend more than their income.

Name withheld

I pay my bills weekly. It takes about 30 minutes. I have only one checking account.

By looking 10 days ahead, I can plan for what's coming due. I have set up a lot of bills to be paid automatically, so I spend less time on bill paying than I did in the past. I have two credit cards, but have never carried a balance. My former husband assumed he would manage our finances. He had been in debt before we were married and the debt continued.

Betsy Roderick, administrative / personnel work. Raised in New Jersey

---

My wife and I sit down together at end of each month and pay the bills. It takes us only about 30 minutes. We have just one checking account. We use Quicken to make it easier.

Don Gruitt, computer programmer, retired. Raised in West Virginia

Chris Gruitt, computer programmer, retired. Raised in Virginia

---

I spend about a half-hour to pay the bills. I do this twice each month. My husband has one checking account, used to pay the bills, and I have one for groceries (and presents!). We've never had more than these two accounts. Currently, he pays the bills. We've used different systems in the past. Sometimes, I paid the bills. Other times, we did it together.

We've never used a budget. If we end up with a lot of bills, then we spend until the bills are paid off! You don't need to spend a lot of time with bill paying to have financial success. We know what we can do, and I think some people never get it. They are "financially challenged" and will never get it. It doesn't take more than an hour per month. The key is not to try to keep up with everyone else, and don't think you have to buy everything that TV says you should have.

Name withheld, 60. Teacher

Paying the bills is simple. You just collect them all month long, then take the stack of bills, open them up, enter Quicken on your PC, and pay from there. It takes about 10 minutes. I've tried every way imaginable to handle bill paying. I used to pay the bills right away, but that's a waste of time—and no one is expecting to get paid right away, anyway. So, now, I do it monthly. I don't even keep the bill stubs anymore!

I don't think dealing with bills and achieving financial success are linked. Spend your efforts with doing a good job at your profession and with investing for the long term, and just don't neglect the bills.

Mike Ferrier, company president and CEO. Raised in north eastern Ohio

Carol Ferrier, volunteer. Raised in Youngstown, Ohio

I pay bills twice a month, just have one checking account, and some bills are paid automatically. It takes about 45 minutes. We used to have two accounts, but we kept making deposits into the wrong account, fouling things up, so we just use one account now.

We've never bothered with a budget. Never needed to . . . we always knew how much we could spend. But we do track our actual expenses. I have a ledger of what I pay, by category— auto expenses, credit cards, dept store expenses, and so on. It helps us stay focused.

Name withheld, homemaker. Raised in Buffalo, New York

Spouse, retired chairman of a hospital's department of medicine

We pay our bills once a month. It doesn't take long—maybe 1–2 hours. We have three checking accounts. One is a money market account, which we maintain for emergencies. The second is a joint checking account, and that's where we pay all the bills from. And my wife has a separate account to use as she pleases. She buys the groceries with that account as well as anything else she wants. We transfer money from the joint account into that account for her, and she also makes money at craft shops, and that money goes into her account as well.

Money is not a "power" issue in our household. Since I'm an accountant, I handle the bill paying. When we first got married 34 years ago, my wife felt guilty asking for money, so we got her a separate checking account, and that takes away the guilt.

I've never bothered with a budget. I'm always aware of what is coming in and going out. For instance, I know the house insurance is due on annual basis and I know I have to come up with money to pay for it. The key is to anticipate and be methodical; be aware of when bills are coming in.

Name withheld, accountant

Spouse, entrepreneur

A way to stay out of debt: I use Quicken and I have in my checking account a phantom account called the reserve account. When I make a charge or buy something from a catalog, I make an entry in my checkbook in Quicken into the phantom account. When the bill comes I cancel the entries and my checkbook is back to where it was. I'm not looking at money I've already spent. The biggest problem with credit card debt is not keeping track of what has been charged and consequently not having the funds to pay the bill. Using my way, the money is set aside as it is charged.

Tony D'Alessandro, electronic engineer. Raised in Wyoming, Pennsylvania

Ruth D'Alessandro, homemaker. Raised in Ayer, Massachusetts

I sit down at the kitchen table once a week and pay whatever bills are due. I label each envelope with date due and amount due as they come in. Then I file them and once a week pay what's in the file. It takes 30–60 minutes.

We have two checking accounts. One is for household bills, for whatever we want to do as a family. My wife uses her own account as she sees fit. I used to maintain three checking accounts, but it's easier to keep track of just one. And there's just one to balance, too!

I've been paying the bills for 48 years. My wife used to do it, but somewhere along the line I complained and she said I could pay them from then on. I've learned to keep my mouth shut since.

Dan Novak, comptroller, retired. Raised in Wall, Pennsylvania

Jeanne Novak, secretary, retired. Raised in Washington, DC

Paying the bills takes only a small amount of time each month because some of our monthly payments are automatically debited from our checking account. We use one checking account, and I place a lot of charges on Visa, to be paid at the end of the month. Our income goes directly into checking, and then we withdraw cash for our weekly expenses. We never charge what we can't pay for at the end of the month. We've never been on a budget, either—we buy only what we need, and we try to save the rest. We don't live beyond our means. Our only debt is the mortgage on the house and our car payment. We never thought of this as "financial success"—it's just something we do every month.

Martin Bell, retired horticulturist. Raised in Silver Spring, Maryland

Martha Bell, office manager. Raised in Silver Spring, Maryland

For 20 years, we paid bills monthly. Now we do it every two weeks. The night before payday, anything due was written out and prepared for mail that day. Since we're paid twice a month, we subtract half of the mortgage amount from our checkbook in the middle of the month, pretending that that money is no longer there. Then, when we get the next paycheck, we subtract the other half of the mortgage and send the entire amount to the mortgage company.

We spend less than an hour paying the bills. Sometimes I do it, sometimes he does it. We switch off after a few months, so the biggest issue is being careful with the mail, so we don't lose any bills that need to be paid. Both of us always are in tune to what is happening. That's critical. I've heard about too many women who don't know what's going on. We've raised five children, and we pass along to them these lessons.

The key is to be organized, disciplined, and to have control over spending. Don't use credit cards, live within your means, and realize that you don't have to have everything right now.

Name withheld, receptionist

Spouse, chief reconnaissance analyst

I write each check a week before the bill is due. I have a record that tells me when the bills are due, with a little chart I've created that's divided into different categories—mortgage, charity, and so on, 10 categories in all—and it shows the date and amount due. Once it's paid, I cross it off the list with a red pencil. This lays it all out and lets me see where we stand during the month. I look at it on almost a daily basis.

It might sound like a lot of work, but it doesn't take very long, just a few minutes a day. I have a sheet for every month. I copy the blank sheet and fill in the numbers as they come along. Why bother with a computer when all I have to do is get out my ledger?

All the bills get paid from one account. My wife has her own account, which she uses for herself.

I handle the bill paying because years ago, my wife got stressed out over it. Paying the bills is easy as long as you have a system. By focusing on when the bills are due, you can make sure you've got enough money. Twenty years ago, I had to use a budget because I traveled worldwide for 90–100 days a year, three or four weeks at a time. My wife was home with the kids, so before I left, I'd leave everything ready to be paid. I'd have a stamp on the envelope, with a date marked on the outside of the envelope so my wife would know when to mail the payment off. I needed to be sure our accounts had enough money to cover the bills. Without such extensive travel anymore, that system isn't needed. But it was easy to see why my wife could get stressed over money!

The key is not to spend more than you have. This is especially important with home buying. Expenses can be unpredictable. If you keep track of your expenditures, you'll be better able to make room for savings.

Peter Callejas, engineer, retired. Raised in Newburyport, Massachusetts

Elizabeth Callejas, secretary, retired. Raised in Amesbury, Massachusetts

---

You always need to know how much you need, but it only takes an hour a month to do it right.

Name withheld, retired Army officer

Spouse, retail sales, retired

I give to the church and to charities before I pay bills. I feel that if you take care of giving first, the rest will come.

Name withheld

I pay bills at the end of every month. Hate it. Takes an hour—an hour too much! I have one credit union account. I charge everything I can, and write just one check at the end of the month. Much easier and quicker. Ten to fifteen years ago, I had two accounts, but didn't need the second one. My wife used to the pay the bills—for the first five years—but she got tired of it, so I do it now. She doesn't want to be bothered with it.

As much as I dislike it, I am adamant about maintaining good credit. (I used to be a credit manager and the benefits of having good credit stuck.) I pay everything on time. Years ago, I used to enjoy the fact that I was able could pay all our bills— it was a sense of accomplishment. Now it's just a chore!

As you can imagine, I've never budgeted. But I have one rule: each month something must go towards the future. Organization is key to success. Anyone who is aware and organized will achieve success. You don't have to like it. You do it anyway.

Frank DeCola, auto sales. Raised in Washington, DC

Kathryn DeCola, teacher. Raised in Alabama

---

§§

I have one checking account, and I pay bills every few days—right while I'm sitting in front of the TV. We tried a budget in the early days, but when we added everything up, we were $11 short. So we just decided not to buy what we couldn't afford. A budget wasn't necessary. Spending a lot of time with financial matters doesn't seem to have much affect on how the investments do, so we spend little time with them. As a Depression Baby, I learned how to stretch things, and being divorced with children I learned how to be in charge and take care of them.

Virgina Endicott, teacher. Raised in Globe, Arizona

We were married in 1943, a year after my husband went into the service. We always used one checking account, and one credit card for the bills. I pay all the bills in the middle of the month, in less than an hour. I type each bill out on a typewriter; my son gave me a computer but I don't know how to use it yet! And I keep all the records on a monthly basis—and I have every check stub we've written since 1959 until my husband retired in 1982. I keep perfect records. But we're not big spenders, so we didn't need a budget.

Gladys L. Mason, homemaker. Raised in Arlington, Virginia

Staying at home was a hard decision and it still is hard. Everybody says you have to make two incomes to survive. When I quit working, Steve was making $40,000 and I was making $32,000. So quitting to stay home—we had one child and another on the way—meant giving up a big chunk of our income.

We looked at what we were spending and saw where we could cut. We refinanced our car loan and mortgage to bring those payments down. We dropped the trash service and cable TV. I read books to help think of more ways to save money. It was hard emotionally because people think you ought to be working. We don't live in a fancy house or drive nice cars, yet others are doing that—and it makes me wonder if I should be back to work. After all, I could earn a good bit of money.

But I don't want to. Even before we were dating, my husband and I had one of our first meaningful conversations. We knew we both wanted me to be home to raise our kids. But when we had our first child, I didn't think we could manage it financially. Before I quit, my boss suggested that I work four days at home and one day at the office each week. But as my son got older, it got harder and quickly became unmanageable. With the second one coming, we didn't want to keep doing that.

So you make compromises and decide what's most important. One of the best things is that I was putting money away since I was 24, and that money is still invested—and it will be until Steve is ready to retire. Starting early really helped us. A friend of mine has cashed in her 401(k) plan three or four times. We've never cashed ours in, and we won't. Seems like most of the world does.

Mary Greer, stay-at-home mom, computer programmer. Raised in Fairfax County, Virginia

Steve Greer, systems engineer. Raised in Vienna, Virginia

§§

My wife was injured, so our finances became tight but are still manageable. I drew up a list of everything we spend every month, as well as those occasional expenses. So now I know when I can be expecting the bills. This helps plan our day-to-day finances. We can also see the months where there will be extra cash that we can put into savings. Also, we pay attention to our credit: Someone stole my wife's credit card and driver's license, so we ended up having bad credit for a time, but that was easily rectified. And, we keep a good supply of emergency money around, just in case—and it came in handy. Don't get greedy and be in a position where you don't have to worry about finances. By saving, you don't have to worry about today or the future.

Name withheld, program manager

Spouse, administrative assistant

§§

If I am going to buy something I don't need, I always try to figure out how much money it would take to earn back the interest for what I am about to spend. It sometimes deters me from making the purchase.

Wilmer Hutchison, insurance agent. Raised in Chantilly, Virginia

When I was a kid I went to Florida, and I was given $5 to spend each day on food, entertainment, etc. I always wanted money left at the end of the day, so it became a game for me to save money—and it still is.

Kathleen Keim, international economist. Raised in Milwaukee, Wisconsin

---

We never had a budget and never set aside a designated amount for savings. We just don't spend. We still don't.

An incident comes to mind. A few years ago, an acquaintance I had not seen in over a year came to our area for a vacation. We met for lunch and then wandered around looking in shop windows. At one store, a pant suit caught her eye and she went in to try it on (this after she had told me during lunch that she needed to start saving some money!) It fit and looked good on her. She asked me if she should buy it. I said, "Do you need it?" She looked at me as if I was speaking Greek and asked me what I meant by "need." She had no idea what I meant. I couldn't understand how she could not understand what "need" meant. I finally defined "need" by asking her if she could imagine any place she could not go or any invitation she could not accept if she did not have that particular pant suit. Wasn't there an article of clothing in her current wardrobe that would fill the same need? She looked at me strangely and asked the saleswoman to hold the pant suit while she thought it over. We walked out and continued discussing the concept of want, like, it fits, and looks good vs. need (especially when trying to save money). In the end, she did not buy the pant suit.

H.B., CPA. Raised in Brooklyn, New York

SECRET #7

Money Management is a Family Affair Involving Their Kids as well as Their Parents.

SECRET #7
Money Management is a Family Affair Involving Their Kids as well as Their Parents.

In many American households, there are three subjects never discussed at the dinner table: politics, sex, and money.

I won't comment on the first two, but the third is fair game. If you fail to talk about money with your family, major problems are likely to result. And yet, few parents discuss the subject with their kids—whether their children are small, or well into adulthood.

The Mistake Made by Parents of School-Age Children

You may not talk to your kids about money, but they're learning about it from you nonetheless.

Think about it. After all, you know kids don't learn about money in school, and while they might learn about sex by sneaking a peek at *Playboy*, they sure don't learn about money by passing around copies of *The Economist*. Face it: your kids learn everything they know about money simply by observing you.

Ask a group of five-year-olds where money comes from. The most common answer you'll hear? *The ATM.* You might think that's a funny answer until you realize the kindergartners are serious. After all, the kids go with you to the automated teller machine, and they watch as you press a few buttons, and they see money pop out. If you don't tell them what's going on, what conclusion must they draw?

A member of my staff once shared with me a story involving her 12-year-old daughter. The staffer had been doing a great job eliminating her credit card debts, and shortly after paying off one such card, she called the department store to cancel the account. Her daughter, overhearing the conversation, was frightened. "But Mom, what if we need to buy clothes?" her daughter cried. "Don't worry," her mom explained. "If we need to buy clothes, we'll just pay cash." Her daughter's eyes opened wide. "Pay cash? I didn't know stores accepted cash," she said.

Before you laugh, ask yourself: when's the last time your child saw you buy something from a clothing or department store with cash?

Do your children understand how money works? How to get it and what to do with it? As I explained in Rule #63 of *The New Rules of Money*[67], you need to teach your kids how money works. Teach them to tithe a portion, save a portion, invest a portion, and enjoy a portion of the money they get, so they learn to love what money can do, and not love money itself.

And when they do get money, be sure that taxes are withheld. Sure! Their boss will withhold taxes when they get a paycheck, so let 'em get used to it. And while you're at it, let 14-year-olds and up help you prepare your tax returns. It's not only a great math lesson, it's a great economics course—as well as a wonderful opportunity to show your kids what's really going on with the family's finances.

But this notion goes back to the concerns people have about telling others how much money they earn. Does the thought of telling your kids how much you earn make you feel embarrassed? Do you feel ashamed to tell your kids how much debt you owe, or how little money you have?

I am not concerned about your embarrassment or shame. I am more concerned that, unless you overcome these feelings, your kids will learn to feel embarrassment and shame about money—because that's what you're teaching them.

---

[67] I'm amazed that my publisher lets me get away with such shameless self-promotion. But, then, considering my publisher published that book, too, maybe it's not so amazing.

The Mistake Made by Parents of Adult Children—Part 1

When you insulate your children from the realities surrounding your finances, they tend to assume you're fine. If my parents are fine, I don't have to worry about them. And beyond all else, parents don't want their kids to worry about them.

Apparently, many parents would prefer that their kids be *shocked*.

Shocked when they discover that their parents are unable to pay their bills. Shocked when they discover they've been named executor of their parent's estate. Shocked to discover how much money Mom and Dad left them.

Such surprises are unfair and unfortunate, yet remarkably common. *My kids don't need to know about my money. I'm fine, and they'll get plenty when the time comes.* This is a common trait, especially among Depression Babies. These folks "went without" for much of their lives. Their parents had nothing, and nothing was expected.

So they expect it to be the same for their kids. But life isn't the same. Many of today's Depression Babies are enjoying a comfortable retirement, and they don't have financial worries. Instead, their biggest financial issues pertain to managing their assets for the remainder of their lives and, ultimately, distributing those assets to their children. And this is where the biggest shocks come.

Too many parents fail—no, *refuse*—to tell their children about their money, even though they fully intend their kids to inherit all of it. Do you think your kids love you only because you have money? If you're right, why would you want to give it to them? And if you're wrong, why the reluctance to discuss it with them?

Indeed, as I relate in *The Truth About Money*[68], keeping secrets about your money is a terrible thing to do to your children. Yet that is precisely what many parents do.

---

[68] Last chance to order! Don't miss out on this exciting opportunity! Visit your favorite bookseller today!

It's bad enough to see parents of grown children create horrible problems in their families, but it's even worse to see problems occur when the parents have tried to avoid them. The cause of most problems? The parents want to be "fair" to their kids.

This almost always causes problems, and for two reasons: first, everyone has a different opinion of what's fair, and second, life simply is not fair. Thus, attempting to handle your money that way is doomed to fail.

Some parents try to be fair by creating a will that leaves equal amounts of money to each child. Usually, that means four children each receive one fourth of a house. Guess what happens when three want to sell but one refuses? Mom and Dad thought they were being fair. What they were really doing was setting the stage for a huge fight among their children.

Actually, make that their children *and their children's spouses.*

I know. Your kids love each other. But do all the in-laws get along? When your two daughters chat on the phone, their husbands might be listening on the extension. When that phone call ends, guess who gets an earful.

Or maybe you plan to disinherit one or more of your children. Have you told them? You need to tell them why—and you need to tell the other children, too. Otherwise, the only thing that's certain is that all your children will equally inherit the family's poor relations.

I've also seen parents leave greater amounts of money to some children than to others—not because they favored one over another, but because some offspring were more financially successful than others. My-son-the-doctor doesn't need my money as much as my-son-the-actor, they sometimes say. But by failing to explain this to their kids, one could inherit nothing but confusion, hurt feelings, and resentment—toward you and his sibling. Along with a desire to contest the will.

All these mistakes are easily avoided. All you have to do is talk with your children. Tell them of your plans and the basis for your decisions. You could discover that you've made some faulty assumptions. And that's the first step to insuring that you do indeed leave the legacy of a happy family.

The Mistake Made by Parents of Adult Children—Part 2

Among my clients is a young couple who was struggling financially. You'd never know it to look at them. Both spouses worked, earning a combined annual income of $85,000. They had three children, and lived in a typical suburban neighborhood. You'd never guess they had $35,000 in credit card debts.

Money was a constant challenge for them. They spent $21,000 in taxes each year, $2,125 a month in mortgage payments ($25,500 annually), $489 monthly for two car payments ($5,868), another $8,000 a year on gasoline and commuting expenses, $10,000 on food, $2,500 on music camp for one child, $3,200 for soccer camp for the other two, and $9,000 to keep three growing kids clothed. There goes $85,000—and not a dime yet spent on insurance, household maintenance, furniture, telephone, or utilities.[69] It's easy to understand why they owed $35,000 to credit cards.[70]

One day, she referred her parents to me. Her dad was a retired Naval officer who spent 15 years as an executive with a telecommunications firm after leaving the service. His wife had retired after 30 years as a schoolteacher. Together, they enjoyed three pensions, joint Social Security benefits—and investment income from their considerable savings. Thanks to generous stock options with his last employer, regular contributions to employer-provided retirement accounts, and regular savings over their entire careers, they had accumulated a portfolio worth $1.4 million. But they still lived just as they had when he was in the Navy and she taught third grade. There was no way they could possibly spend all the money they earned each year, nor did they try to. And their plan, naturally, was to leave everything to their daughter and her family.

---

[69] Or a Friday night pizza.
[70] Please note that although I *understand* it, I do not *approve* of it. These folks were living a lifestyle they couldn't afford. Getting them to realize this was my biggest challenge.

I knew the daughter's situation. I knew the parents' situation. And I knew that neither knew much about the other's finances. *Dad's retired military and Mom's a former teacher*, the daughter said with a shrug. *They seem to be doing fine*, said the parents to me.

Did I tell each about the other? And if I did, how did each react?

You won't find any answers here, because the answers don't matter.[71] The questions that really count are these:

If you were the parent:

would it be better if you knew about your child's situation?

would it be better if the child knew about your situation?

If you were the daughter:

would it be better if your parents knew about your situation?

would it be better if you knew about your parents' situation?

So, I ask you: when's the last time you talked with your kids and your parents about money?

One final comment. This situation isn't limited to generational relationships. I've even seen incredible secrets exist between *spouses*. One case stands out. A woman visiting my web site asked me for help. Here's what she wrote:

Dear Ric,

My husband and I were married six years ago. Before we were married my husband owed the IRS $85,000 in taxes. When we were married I did not know that and so our first year we filed joint. I am now being held accountable for the money that he owes. Is there any way that we can file separate and I not be responsible for something that happened before we were married?

---

[71] This ain't *The Jerry Springer Show*.

Clearly, a relationship with this many secrets has a lot more wrong with it than just money. But money is perhaps one of the most tangible problems a couple might experience.

The Mistake Made by Adult Children

Maybe Dad refuses to get rid of that ratty old chair because he loves it—or maybe he can't afford a new one. How do you know until you have a frank conversation with Dad about his finances—including a look at his bank account statements and tax returns? Do you know if Dad is even *filing* a tax return?

I've seen clients suddenly discover that their parents are deeply in debt—despite their protests that "I'm fine!" For a moment, think about your parents' lifestyle. Have they stopped doing things they used to love? Perhaps they cancelled club memberships. There could be lots of reasons—perhaps they can't afford it anymore. Are house repairs unattended? Are they failing to fill prescriptions? Is there plenty of food in the house? For everyone, it's worth a thought. For some, an inquiry. For others, a full-blown investigation. Do it now—for their sake and for your peace of mind.

And if it will serve as any guide, please know that successful families talk openly about their finances. Of my survey's respondents, 87% have children,[72] and of these, 82% have told their kids about their financial and estate plans. A majority of the remaining 18% have not done so merely because their children are too young (preschoolers or grade schoolers) for such detailed conversations.

---

[72] There goes another excuse for why you aren't rich. Many people blame their lack of money on the costs of raising children. But as you see, nearly nine of out 10 of my firm's clients have kids—and it didn't prevent any of them from getting rich. Start looking for another excuse.

And 46% of my respondents have at least one parent or in-law still living. Of this group, nearly two-thirds know of their parent's financial situation and estate plans.[73]

If you fear that questions about money will be difficult, know that talking about money is one of the best ways to evaluate the strength and depth of a relationship. It will also help you, your parents, and your children achieve greater financial success.

And who knows, if you survive the conversation, you might even start talking about politics and sex.

---

[73] Although still a strong majority, this is the weakest result of my entire survey. I ascribe this relatively low result to the fact that although my clients might want to talk about money with their parents and in-laws, they are afterall the children in this situation, and they must respect their elders' wishes. And today's older generation were raised in an era when these things were never discussed with children. Hence, "only" 63% of my clients have succeeded in talking with their parents about their parents' money.

SUCCESSFUL INVESTORS:
MONEY MANAGEMENT IS A FAMILY AFFAIR INVOLVING THEIR KIDS AS WELL AS THEIR PARENTS.
" IN THEIR OWN WORDS "

Since my father wasn't an investor in anything other than savings accounts, I didn't pursue investment knowledge until a few years prior to my first child entering college. I have found this to be very common. Despite an undergraduate degree in physics and a master's degree in engineering and being professionally licensed, it has amazed me how many of my peers who have analytical skills for working with numbers, calculations, graphs, etc., have such little knowledge when it comes to applying those skills to their own finances! For example, we taught our kids that "small and early equals late and large." I learned the math in engineering economics, but didn't personally apply it until after taking a personal finance class!

Parents aren't doing their children any favors by buying them whatever they want whenever they want it. It's no wonder that when two people who have been given everything all their lives marry, that they will have a tough time staying together when trying to make it on their own.

Our policy for kids: we buy the needs, you add to it for the wants. For example, we'll spend "x" dollars for sneakers; if the kids want to add "x" more dollars to get the neon ones that light up when they walk, that's fine. They have to come up with the money themselves. Our kids have learned that saving for something you want and buying it with your own money makes you appreciate it more when you get it, and it prevents impulse buying when you're older.

Bob and Betsy Werner

I have four kids and all are married. Ages are 35, 33, 29, and 25. All of them know about our finances and estate plans. It's common knowledge. We talk about it, they talk about it—very freely. And we always have: We've talked about our finances with our kids since they were in Junior High School. It's never been a secret. We talked about debt, saving, etc., in the hopes that they'd learn from seeing us handle our money.

My mother is 82, and we know about her finances and she knows about ours. My mom volunteered the information and wanted to know where I stood. My sister knows about my mother's estate too. It took two meetings (for my mother to tell us about her finances). My sister doesn't want to know that stuff, though—her attitude is very different, and she thinks our mom is going to live forever.

My in-laws are very private, though, and we have little or no idea what's going on with them. We ask, but they don't tell. Recently, they sold part of their property and didn't tell us. As it turned out we would've loved to have bought that property from them . . . but they only told us after the fact.

I learned something from my parents, but not from advice they gave me. I learned from their actions . . . they were poor and in debt because they owned no investments. My parents were frivolous with money and I learned not to be frivolous. I think you should keep close tabs on what your parents are doing because they can be taken in a heartbeat. Direct your parents to good financial advice if you can't give it to them yourself.

If I could go backwards in time, I'd tell my parents to share with your children what's going on much earlier than they did.

Joseph Ivers, director of a church's Adult Christian Education Program. Raised in Watertown, New York

Connie Cummings, director of a church's Child Enrichment Program

We have three sons, ages 38, 35, and 32—two are married. They all know about our finances and estate plans—they all have a copy of our documents, in fact. It was a casual meeting and they were fine about learning the information and they appreciated our thoughtfulness.

We started talking to our kids about money early, when they were in grade school.

My Dad is 91 and my mom is 86. I have a copy of their estate plans and finances—you have to know about their plans because at some point in time you will be faced with it.

Robert Montgomery, 63, retired electrical engineer, now a real estate agent. Raised in Grove City, Pennsylvania

Elizabeth Montgomery, 62, former teacher, now a real estate agent

---

I have one daughter, who's 30 and unmarried. When she went to college, we talked about her needing to work during the summers to help pay for college. When she graduated, we talked about job security, pensions plans, and saving for the future. Recently, we've been talking about investing because she's coming into some money from an inheritance. If I could go backwards in time, I would've had more and more talks about money with my daughter.

Robert Warren, consulting actuary. Raised in Buffalo, New York

Christine Warren, homemaker

I have three children, all married, and my wife has three children, also all married. My kids are 40, 38, and 31, and my wife's children are 43, 41, and 38. We each have seven grandchildren.

My wife and I were married in 1996 and we signed a prenuptial agreement. My kids know about my finances and my wife's kids know about hers. My kids have always been part of the decision making with finances in the family.

My mom is 90 years old. She has handled her finances very successfully. Every quarter she informs me of her finances. She even sends my children quarterly statements. Recently, one of her stocks—something she bought after World War II—paid out a dollar, so she called everyone to let them know. The long distance calls cost more than that dollar!

When I was growing up, my dad taught me about making money. He had me working in the meat packing industry when I was eight years old, and he paid me 10 cents an hour. I worked after school and if I was late my dad docked 10 cents from my pay. I learned how to make and spend money and I learned that I didn't want to be at the low end of the totem pole. I wanted out of the meat packing business. The best advice I got from my parents about money was to know where it is coming from and know where it's going. I still follow this advice. When I went to college, they paid for it and when I got out of college, I paid them back. My mother had ledger books dating back to 1938 that included such things as 3-cent stamps, the cost of checks, pair of shoes, etc.

You definitely need to involve kids in the economics of the family, to make them aware of how hard it is to earn a buck. Kids need to understand that they are part of the economics of the family, and they need to know how money is earned and spent. My kids were all given a certain amount of money each year to go to school and when they wanted more, they would come back to the family to discuss the budget. If they borrowed some extra, they would need to repay it. This way, they learned how to budget and make decisions.

Herb Mendelsohn, retired manager. Raised in Pittsburgh, Pennsylvania

When you give kids an allowance make sure they save some of it. Teach them to save.

Joe Schuck, retired federal government employee,
Department of Defense. Raised in St. Paul, Minnesota

Pat Schuck, computer specialist

I have two children that are 35 and 28. My daughter is divorced and my son is married.

We didn't talk a lot about money with my kids until they became teenagers. My son wanted money to buy sports equipment. At the time I was managing the building where we lived—I suggested to my kids that if they wanted to buy extra things, why don't we take on the cleaning of the building ourselves, as a family thing, rather than paying an outside cleaning lady. That was the turning point. Both my children developed a wonderful work ethic.

When I was growing up, my mom was poor. We lived with my grandfather. I remember when I was seven or eight years old, I went to the company store and charged a silk nightgown for my mother's birthday. My mother was mortified and told me that we couldn't afford it—I was crushed. That's when I learned about finances. I don't think I ever got much advice about money from my mom or grandfather.

Name withheld, secretary

I have three boys—37, 35, and 31—they are all married. My boys have all been involved with the trusts I've set up. It was a formal meeting and then dinner followed. We have lots of dinners at our house, I think it's important. They were very interested in the trusts and contributed their ideas and thoughts.

I started an IRA for my youngest in 1982. I put $60 into a bank account—now, it's worth only $104. Andrew says he won't do anything with it because it's his inheritance. We all get a big laugh out of it.[74]

Frank J. Massaro, retired police officer. Raised in Milford, Massachusetts

Marie Ann Massaro, homemaker, which Frank stressed is
"a very important and vital position." Raised in Franklin, Massachusetts

§§

We have one son who is 36 and married. He pretty much knows about our finances and estate plans. I'm in financial management myself, so I've helped him out with his taxes and he's seen what we have. We've included my son in everything because when he was young, my husband was gone a lot with his work and we wanted to be sure our son knew our finances— he's our one and only.

He was in elementary school when we started giving him a small allowance. We wanted to impress on him the importance of saving. He opened a bank account and bought savings bonds when he got a little older. My parents told me to never spend everything that you had coming in; always save something first. Pay yourself first and get into the habit of saving. I've tried to pass that advice along to my son.

Name withheld, retired from military

---

[74] Andrew is a Certified Financial Planner with Edelman Financial Services, Inc.

I have four children, ages 27 to 35. We talked to our children about our estate plans when we put everything into trusts. I got together a little briefing and we sat the kids down and told them about it.

My mother will be 100 in May. She's taken both my sister and I aside and told us everything. I have access to her checking accounts and I have her power of attorney. She is very well organized.

It's important that you spend time with your parents and children so they know what's going on.

Name withheld, retired personnel director

Spouse, retired bank employee

I have two children, ages 22 and 24—neither are married, both are still in college. Their grandmother has given them money over the years, which has been put into investments. Their grandmother also gave each of them a book called *The Richest Man in Babylon* by George S. Clason. It's a short little book that talks about dividing your money into three parts— long term savings, paying debts, and discretionary money. It's been a big help to our kids. They put aside money into savings each month.

After each child earned certain grades in school, they got a new car—but there was a kicker. They have to pay us back $50 per month while they are in school. The money goes into a mutual fund account. We're encouraging them to save and not buy another new car until they have enough in their fund to pay cash for their next car.

Our kids know about our estate plans. They know that if something were to happen to my husband and me now, they wouldn't inherit any money until they are 35—unless it's needed for medical expenses or an emergency.

My husband's mother is 87 and sharp as a tack. She has a good amount of money and she keeps my husband very much informed of her financial situation. She sends him documents regularly. Money is her hobby—her favorite magazine is *Forbes*.

My parents taught me not to spend money I haven't got, and my attitude about money doesn't differ that much from theirs. Right now, we could afford to move into a more expensive home, but we don't. We don't belong to the country club, buy new or luxury cars, and we don't travel first class.

If I could go backwards in time, I wouldn't change anything regarding our kids and money. They inherited good money sense from their grandmother.

Name withheld, homemaker and former teacher

Dad told me stories about The Great Depression, about how little there was and no opportunity to work. Kids were expected to work to support the family. My father-in-law told me that one year, his Christmas present was an orange. When my dad came home from WWII, he won some money and because of the Depression, he put it into the bank. He could have bought some ocean front, but he lived through some very rough times, and grew afraid to take a lot of risk. So I learned about the stock market on my own.

Jay, lobbyist

Sharon, art teacher

My mother came from Greece after World War II with a $20 bill and she still has the $20. My mom and her sister bought Coca-Cola and other company stocks and their money grew. That's how I saw money grow. My dad is terrible with investing. He was six or seven years old during the Depression, and his father—my grandfather—lost six of seven restaurants during the Crash. My mother set up a dress shop and bought rental buildings—and she never had a high school education. My dad, though, has an MBA from Wharton and made good money as an ad executive and never saved—never invested in the stock market. My mom did all the investing and saving. Now they're retired and if they have any money left over it's because of her.

Name withheld, screenwriter

Spouse, journalist

I inherited a farm, and I didn't know I was the heir. I've tried, and I can't sell it. It's a pain because I have to pay taxes on it. Didn't realize how much of a pain it could be to inherit land.

Name withheld

We set up trusts for our kids, and it's been very satisfying. By contrast, when my mother-in-law's estate was settled, one of my wife's sisters was accused of fraud and the case ultimately involved lawyers in four states. That's not worth any price.

Name withheld

My daughter is a fourth grade teacher. She pays her students in Monopoly money for doing their homework, and especially for extra homework and unassigned classroom work. They are given the choice to invest the money in her mutual funds or put it in the class bank. At the end of each week, they must compute the amount they have earned along with the interest and keep a record of the total. Sometimes, this is a loss, since they must pay her double if they fail to complete homework assignments.

At the end of a three-month period, she has an auction (selling stuff that's important to fourth graders) where the students bid using their earnings.

When they were studying the Depression, she told them they had lost all the money—what a reaction she got! It helped them understand a little better what some of their grandparents had gone through during that era. After they sweated a few days, she returned the money—but that's another story.

Ethel Perkins, retired. Raised in Washington, DC

My mother would give me a quarter a week when I was a little girl. I had to put 10 cents in the collection plate on Sunday; five cents went to my piggy bank to save; I was allowed to spend five cents to buy candy at school (candy cost 1 cent then, so that bought one piece of candy per day); and the last five cents would be used on anything I wanted. Over the years my allowance—and eventually my income—increased, but the concept always remained the same.

Barbara Brown

We've set up accounts for our grandkids for college. One of them is three years old and she has about $38,000 in there already. It ought to be a substantial amount of money by the time she's 18 years old. I've told my daughter to set up an account for her and let money sit for many years.

Name withheld, international sales

Spouse, housewife

I have a daughter who is as poor as a church mouse. She is a single mom, lives in a trailer, has two teenage boys, and yet she still manages to put $25 into a mutual fund each month. I think that's great.

Fran Laux, 60. computer systems analyst, retired. Raised in Los Angeles, California

---

I was talking with my 12-year-old daughter, Dakoda, about the need to save, and she summarized our conversation by saying, "A dollar a day will make you rich when you're old and gray." I thought that was cute.

Robin Thompson, AXYS manager

SECRET #8

They Differ From Most Investors in the Attention They Pay to the Media.

SECRET #8
They Differ From Most Investors in the Attention They Pay to the Media.

In order to succeed, you need information. Where do investors get it? It's simple.

They start each day with *The Wall Street Journal* and *Investors Business Daily* to track market activity, *The Washington Post* for political and national news and *The New York Times* for business and international news. Then they tune to CNBC all day, occasionally flipping to Bloomberg, CNN, and MSNBC.

They catch up on the day's events they may have missed by watching PBS' *Nightly Business Report*.

Each Friday, they read *Barrons* and *Business Week*, and tune into to PBS' *Wall Street Week* with Louis Ruykeser.

Twice a month, they scour *Forbes* and *Fortune*.

Monthly reading consists of *Money*, *Smart Money*, *Worth*, *Bloomberg Personal*, *Kiplinger's Personal Finance*, and half a dozen assorted hot-tips newsletters.

They belong to the local chapter of the Individual Investors Association of America and faithfully attend each monthly meeting.

They download their portfolios daily, sometimes hourly if things are really moving, and they know more about the Dow's standing than today's temperature.

But you don't do any of these things. Why not? Because

a. You don't have the time

b. You find the subject incredibly boring

c. You haven't a clue as to what all those people are talking about

Choose from a, b, or c. Some people will choose them all. It doesn't matter, for each is sufficient to explain why you don't pay much attention to what's going on in the world of finance. But your lack of attention doesn't explain why you're not successful—because most of America's financially successful people don't pay any more attention to this stuff than you do.

It's true. According to our survey results, only 19% read *The Wall Street Journal*; only 21% watch CNBC or PBS' *Wall Street Week*, and less than 20% attended a financial seminar in the past year. Barely 15% read one or more personal finance magazines and only 11% watch PBS' *Nightly Business Report*. Eight percent or less read investment tips newsletters, business newspapers, or magazines, tune in to financial radio or TV shows, or frequent financial on-line sites.[75] The rest—from 79% to 99% of our clients, depending on the medium in question—do none of the above. Yet they're financially successful anyway.

So if you think you're not doing well with money because you're unplugged, you need to find another excuse. Like all the other excuses we've covered in this book, this one won't do, either.

In fact, a strong case can be made that the people who *don't* pay attention are more likely to succeed—if only because they avoid information overload. Too many neophytes visit internet chat rooms and bulletin boards, where they engage in conversation with people whose names they don't know, listen to tips about stocks they've never heard of, trade rumors about things they don't understand, and buy shares in companies without first verifying any of the information they've been given.

Too many do-it-yourselfers scan the personal finance magazines, where typical issues contain as many as 40 investment tips; that's 500 in a year. They read newspaper columns that cover the Wall Street beat. Each column features as many as 10 stocks; that's another 500 tips a year, multiplied by hundreds of writers.

---

[75] Excluding my offerings, of course!

Television shows parade money managers, investment advisors, journalists, and economists across the screen every day. Each offers as many as five "hot tips" in an appearance; that's thousands of tips a year.

More than 300 investment newsletters are available by subscription; each offers one to 50 tips in every issue. Some even offer daily hot lines.

Dozens of get-rich-quick artists offer books, tapes, and seminars, often charging thousands of dollars to show you their investment strategies.

All this despite the fact that Warren Buffett, the world's most successful investor, says that the best investors might be able to come up with 10 to 20 great ideas in a *lifetime*.

If you're trying to achieve financial success, avoid what my firm's clients avoid, and do as they do.

My firm's clients avoid following the market too closely, and they largely avoid the avalanche of information that's continually produced by the markets and the media.

What they do instead is invest as much money as they can, as often as they can, and for as long as they can. If you'll do the same, you too will become wealthy.

SUCCESSFUL INVESTORS:
THEY DIFFER FROM MOST INVESTORS IN THE ATTENTION THEY PAY TO THE MEDIA.
" IN THEIR OWN WORDS "

I would say I probably spend around seven hours per week reading about and watching TV on personal finances. I read the business section of the *Washington Post* and the *Washington Times*. I also watch the business news on TV and that's about it.

I find the subject of personal finance a chore. I don't subscribe to any financial pubs because I leave all that stuff to my advisor. I stay out of the stock market because in the past, whenever I got in, I always made mistakes. I'm not hindered by this, though. I just have no time or interest in personal finance. And I certainly don't make any decisions based on the media.

Jim Elliott, public relations specialist, retired. Raised in New Mexico and Montana on Indian reservations, dad was a doctor who helped Native Americans.

Jane Elliott, housewife, works part-time as a cashier at a school

---

For me, personal finance is more of a chore than a hobby, and the media gives both good and bad advice, so I don't rely on the media. And I've never bought an investment based on a hot tip. Instead, I invest for the long term and seek good advice about where to put my money.

Kenneth R. Gossage, retired from AT&T. Raised in Arlington, Virginia

The financial media is boring, so I don't read or tune in. I don't believe the media offers good advice. They have an agenda. In fact, I did once buy an investment based on a hot tip. Back in the 1980s, I read about a tip in a personal finance magazine. It sounded so good. I knew nothing about the investment but I told my daughter about it and she bought me 50 shares for my birthday; it was a penny stock, so it wasn't too expensive. Well, in three months, the company went belly up. But I still have the certificate showing the number of shares I own. It's a constant reminder not to make the same mistake again.

Fran Laux, computer systems analyst, retired. Raised in Los Angeles, California

---

I don't spend any time tuning into the media about personal finance. If you're investing for the long term, what's the point of studying the daily Dow reports?

I don't consider personal finance to be either a chore or a hobby. Personal finance is a responsibility. So I don't base financial decisions on what I read or hear in the media—you might as well make decisions by reading your horoscope! Certainly when I make a decision, it's based on research and the input from my advisor, and then I make up my own mind.

Bill Erbach, Sr., clergyman. Raised in Kearny, New Jersey

Martha Erbach, professor of nursing. Raised in Suffolk, Virginia

---

I spend less than 15 minutes per week tuning into the personal finance media. I don't just use the media for hot tips— I use them as a basis for information and then I talk to experts.

Tim, sales

I don't spend much time at all tuning into the media because I don't have the time. I'm only interested enough so I can avoid not having money when I retire . . . when I was in high school, my grandma was two years away from retirement when her company folded and along with it went her pension. This was in the days before there were laws to protect pensions. My grandfather had never worked anywhere long enough to have a pension plan, and I remember the atmosphere of the conversations between my parents and grandparents. My grandparents were concerned about how they were going to live because the only thing they had for retirement was social security. It was a shock to everybody. I don't want to end up like that—it was a real motivation seeing something like this happen in the family.

Name withheld, website designer

I've learned that the media doesn't offer good advice, so I don't base my decisions on the media or hot tips.

Name withheld, manager

I've learned to stay for the long course, and not to let the interim "noise" from the news interrupt you from sticking with your plan.

John W. Roberts, financial analyst. Raised in Kalamazoo, Michigan

In Their Own Words

The Biggest Mistake I Ever Made

The Biggest Mistake I Ever Made

Lack of investments early on. Also, I bought whole life insurance . . . I thought whole life would be a wonderful savings idea. It wasn't.

Michael F. Burke, retired from the Air Force, now working as a defense analyst with a large technical corporation. Born in Saratoga Springs, New York

Elinor K. Burke, former Air Force nurse, now a printmaker. Born in Springfield, Massachusetts

---

I didn't start investing early enough. I waited until I was 46 because I didn't know what to do, so I did nothing.

Jackie Peluso, federal government employee. Raised in Rockville, Maryland

---

My biggest mistake: Not investing in stocks sooner.

Name withheld, business automation consultant

Spouse, law enforcement

Not seeking advice of a planner a lot sooner.

John Barrow, public safety employee. Raised in Columbia, Maryland

Not saving the maximum amount I could have by law. When I came out of college and was earning money, well, in your early 20s it's easy-come-easy-go, and I didn't appreciate the importance of compounding interest over multiple years. I also wasn't focused on retirement.

David Webb, executive with a gas industry research organization. Raised in Lubbock, Texas

Jean Webb, homemaker. Raised in Arab, Alabama

My biggest mistake? Not starting sooner.

Jim McDaniel, park manager. Raised in Boston, Massachusetts

Michele McDaniel, administrative assistant. Raised in Lowell, Massachusetts

---

Investing in oil wells in Texas. I still get a check every month. But I had four of them, and three stopped producing. It's not what I expected from my $40,000 investment, but I think I've broken even. You win some and you lose some.

Heinrich Hofmann, caterer. Raised in Persenbeug, Austria

Anna R. Hofmann, caterer. Raised in Minas Gerais, Brazil

Recently, I purchased a condo which was too small. I need to have something bigger and now I need to get rid of this one, and I am selling it for a loss.

Marty C., secretary. Raised in McAlester, Oklahoma

I once paid off the mortgage on a former house we owned. It would have been better to invest that money.

Bea Blacklow, epidemiologist. Raised in Elmont, Long Island

Roger Blacklow, political coordinator. Raised in Washington, DC

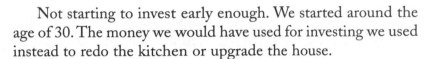

Not starting to invest early enough. We started around the age of 30. The money we would have used for investing we used instead to redo the kitchen or upgrade the house.

Stephanie Thomas, information officer at U.S. Department of Agriculture. Raised in Springfield, Virginia

Brad Thomas, computer analyst. Raised in Vienna, Virginia

I bought a mutual fund a week before the Crash of 1987. I put $12,000 in and lost $3,000 in a week. But it eventually recovered.

Tony D'Alessandro, electronic engineer. Raised in Wyoming, Pennsylvania

Ruth D'Alessandro, homemaker. Raised in Ayer, Massachusetts

Not filing my income taxes for a few years, and they caught me. Thanks to my financial planner I was able to overcome this.

William Hillman, formerly with U.S. Department of Education. Raised in Paulsboro, New Jersey

Helen Hillman, municipal worker, retired. Raised in New River, Virginia

Not trying to save for retirement earlier. I started late and really had to work hard to play catchup.

Willis H. Martin, systems engineer. Raised in New Freedom, Pennsylvania

Marcia G. Martin, travel agent. Raised in York, Pennsylvania

Not saving early enough. When you're young and foolish you don't think about saving. I saved most of my money in the last 15 years instead of starting younger.

Charles Canard, retired, widowed. Raised in Warrenton, Virginia

We added my wife's name to some of my father-in-law's accounts. That was a mistake because, at his death, we incurred capital gains taxes unnecessarily. Never put a child's name on a parent's account.

Pat Black, computer programmer. Raised in Baltimore, Maryland

Buying our house, because I borrowed money from my 401(k) to do it. I know now that's a humongous mistake, because of the impact on my retirement. But, I wised up and paid off the loan and put the money back into my 401(k).

Name withheld, business consultant. Raised in Tempe, Arizona

Spouse, physician. Raised in Tulsa, Oklahoma

My biggest mistake was in not saving enough. I started to put money away when I was single, even had some stocks. I was a federal government employee on the west coast, then transferred to Washington, DC, and then back to the west coast. I thought I was on top of my career, but we weren't saving. I should have stayed on the initial plan of plugging away, paying myself first. I'm telling my kids now to do that— to invest now and let the money work for you. I'm trying to get them to set up a portfolio now, while they're young.

Howard Gaidsick, middle management with the U.S. Government. Raised in Seattle, Washington

Barbara Gaidsick, registered nurse. Raised in Baltimore, Maryland

Not investing in retirement sooner, I was about 35 when I started investing in an IRA and at that point you could deduct it from your taxes. That's when I started . . . I wished I had started sooner.

Shirley Hurst, registered nurse. Raised in Hanover, Pennsylvania

We bought a timeshare and we are trying to unload it.

Bill Harper, retail manager. Raised in McKeesport, Pennsylvania

Shirley Harper, executive secretary. Raised in Front Royal, Virginia

My biggest mistake was not saving sooner in life. In the early years, I took $5 out of my paycheck each week to put into a mutual fund. The money sat there and grew so much that I was able to use it for a down payment on my first house! I never knew anything about finances, but I was lucky and took advantage of the compounding of interest.

Charles Hottel, computer specialist. Raised in Suitland, Maryland

---

We would have been much better off if we had started investing at 30 instead of 50.

Neil Walp, retired regional economic planner. Raised in Bloomsburg, Pennsylvania

Mary Walp, retired credit analyst. Raised in Lightstreet, Pennsylvania

---

Not investing sooner and not investing more.

Fred D., project executive. Raised in San Mateo, California

Shelley D., self-employed project manager. Raised in Hillsdale, New Jersey

---

Subscribed to a newsletter. Then the author started a mutual fund and I put in $15,000. The first six months went well, but in the second six months it went down the toilet. I was lucky to get out with $9,000. The lesson is, know who you are dealing with.

Florian Hocke, retired rocket scientist (for real). Raised in Brooklyn, New York

Not investing earlier.

Name withheld, software engineer. Raised in Woodbridge, Virginia

---

I don't think I started early enough. I should have started as soon as I was out of school and had my first job.

Name withheld, project manager. Raised in Allen Park, Michigan

Spouse, Teacher

I followed some advice from a friend to invest in real estate. This was about 10 or 15 years ago, and it didn't work out. The market was hot at the time I got the advice, then two years later it went down. I don't do impulse decisions anymore.

Friedel Groene, vice president in charge of electronic hardware manufacturing. Raised in Germany

---

My biggest mistake: I did not invest in mutual funds early enough.

Name withheld, 51. attorney. Raised in Westchester County, New York

Spouse, 48. school librarian

Not participating in the company's 401(k) plan from my first day on the job.

Mark Danisewicz, Chief Financial Officer of major corporation Kinnelon, New Jersey

Karen A. Danisewicz, homemaker. Raised in Springfield, Virginia

---

I should have started sooner. I should have ignored the prejudices against women investing money and should have started investing in mutual funds. Back in 1974, I had $5,000 that I wanted to invest, so I tried calling a couple of brokerage firms, but neither returned my calls. Some of my male co-workers called the same firms and received calls back. Looking back, there was a prejudice against women investing money. No one would take women seriously as an investor, but my male coworkers were taken seriously. So I went to CDs instead. I didn't maximize my savings as well as I could have.

Linda Jackie, computer systems auditor, Department of the Navy. Raised in Falls Church, Virginia

---

I kept a great deal of savings in CDs as opposed to seeking professional advice on how I might better invest it.

Kathleen Hoyt, retired, former deputy director for inspections in the U.S. Government. Raised in Columbia, Missouri

---

My biggest mistake was not starting early enough . . . I should have started as soon as I was an adult and working.

Charles Duttweiler, publisher at trade association. Raised in Ridgewood, New York

Dolores Dutweiler, homemaker. Raised in Ridgewood, New York

We didn't get financial help of the right kind soon enough. We went to a broker but didn't get help. If we had gotten better advice we would have been better off.

Name withheld, auditor

Getting involved with penny stocks.

Dick Ives, retired Naval Officer. Raised in Wellsville, New York

Pat Ives, secretary. Raised in Spencer, Wisconsin

Stay away from rental properties.

Dick Amann, proposal writing consultant. Raised in Long Island, New York

Pidge Amann, company president. Raised in Alexandria, Virginia

---

I wouldn't buy savings bonds. Put that money into mutual funds instead.

Max Thomas, retired Army Officer and consultant. Raised in Indiana.

Dennisse Thomas, registered nurse and housewife. Raised in Indiana

---

Co-signed a loan with somebody who was irresponsible and I ultimately had to pay the loan.

Kathleen Keim, international economist. Raised in Milwaukee, Wisconsin

Bought limited partnerships in oil and cattle.

Jim Irons, Army Officer, retired. Raised in Dayton, Ohio

June, sales. Dayton, Ohio

Wished I had saved my increases in salary instead of spending it.

Name withheld, director of administrative services, retired

Spouse, secretary, retired

When I got $14,000 from my profit-sharing plan, we spent some of it instead of investing it.

Raymond Cogswell, product consultant. Raised in Washington, DC

Betty Cogswell, senior bookkeeper. Raised in Washington, DC

If I could go backward in time, I'd definitely change some things . . . getting married and trusting my former husband to make real estate investments to plan for our retirement was something I wish I could change. He told me not to open IRAs because the real estate investments would be our retirement. Our situation changed, we got divorced, the real estate investments failed, and my former husband went into bankruptcy. That's when I found out that, when we were married, he had forged my name on business loans. I ended up spending the next seven years (after the divorce) being sued by various organizations and paying off my former husband's debts. In retrospect, I probably should have filed for bankruptcy, too—then I could have avoided all the law suits, debts, and lawyer fees. I asked one lawyer how I could have avoided all this and he told me "by being independently wealthy."

So, my biggest mistake was not putting more money aside for my personal retirement and not looking out for myself more.

Karen S. Griffin, executive assistant. Raised in Newton, Massachusetts

---

I listened to a personal friend who wanted to sell me insurance. I bought insurance for the wrong reasons.

Lillian Brown, adjunct professor at Georgetown University. Raised in Huntsville, Ohio

---

Not saving soon enough.

Jovita Franco, sales representative. Raised in Manila, Philippines

Don Franco, veterinarian. Raised in Trinidad, West Indies

I've bought investments based on hot tips. Once, I bought stock in a company that was making a tape recording device and it was going to beat the world and it didn't. Another time I bought on a tip that the guy who invented the helicopter was starting up something, and they said it would sweep the world and it didn't. I don't pay attention to hot tips anymore—these investments were my biggest mistakes.

Jim Elliott, public relations specialist, retired. Raised in New Mexico and Montana on Indian reservations, dad was a doctor who helped Native Americans.

Jane Elliott, housewife, works part-time as a cashier at a school

We wasted money when we were young, buying things we didn't need.

Joseph Rogers, manufacturing coordinator. Raised in Louisa, Virginia

Edna Rogers, secretary. Raised in Demarest, New Jersey

We started out in investing our savings in CDs instead of equities.

Ernie Hubbard, engineer. Raised in North Carolina

Jeanne Hubbard, real estate sales assistant. Raised in Minnesota

---

I owned too much of one stock, and didn't listen to a financial planner's advice to sell some of it to help diversify my portfolio.

Name withheld, systems manager

Spouse, retired secretary

I once did a friend's relative a favor by investing with him. But he gave bad investment advice.

Barbara Ramee, travel accounting administrator. Raised in Meriden, Connecticut

---

I invested in a franchise and lost $25,000—and that $25,000 was borrowed money that I had to repay. I trusted my lawyers. It was a chinese restaurant franchise—they took my $25,000 for franchise fees and were about to take another

$65,000 for equipment, when my wife said, "Let's take a look at it again . . ." Just then, the outfit declared bankruptcy. There is no easy money out there; you have to be careful who you are dealing with.

Joseph Ivers, director of a church's Adult Christian Education Program. Raised in Watertown, New York

Connie Cummings, director of a church's Child Enrichment Program. Raised in Litchfield, Connecticut

My mother-in-law buys high and sells low.

Name withheld

I put too much money into the stock of the company I worked for. Fortunately, it didn't go bankrupt.

Richard W. Voelker, research scientist. Raised in Plainview, Nebraska

Rella S. Voelker, housewife. Raised in Mill Creek, West Virginia

I didn't start investing early enough.

Richard Six, aerospace and electronics. Raised in Miami, Florida

When my mother passed away, we got hammered on taxes because we did some dumb things. When she was in the advanced stages of Alzheimer's Disease, we transferred her house into my brother's name and mine. We did this because we were afraid that her assets might be subject to estate taxes. But our strategy forced us to pay huge capital gains tax, because my mother's house was worth $29,000 when she bought it, and we sold it for $250,000—that meant we had to pay taxes on a $221,000 profit! If we had bothered to get good financial, tax, and legal advice, we could have avoided this huge expense.

Andy Taylor, retired Officer, United States Marines. Currently an 8th grade social studies teacher. Raised in Camden and Margate, New Jersey

Phyllis Taylor, registered nurse, retired. Raised in Trenton, New Jersey

---

I've worked for four different employers in my life, and each had a retirement plan. My biggest mistake was when I left one of the jobs. I took the money out of the plan and instead of saving it for retirement, we used it for immediate cash rather than for our future.

Jack McGaughy, computer analyst, retired. Wyomissing, Pennsylvania

Loy McGaughy, desktop publisher

I would have handled my money differently earlier. We worked with a financial planner earlier, but in retrospect, he was too conservative. Even though we didn't have a lot of money to begin with, we were younger and could have been more aggressive in our investments.

Rosemarie Assad, biochemist and homemaker. Raised in Moorestown, New Jersey

Daniel Abe Assad, periodontist. Raised in Donora, Pennsylvania

I bought into a multi-level marketing program, which turned out to be a scam.

Robert L. Adams, retired Army Officer and retired human resources manager. Raised in Joplin, Missouri, and many places as an "Army Brat"

Lucile Overton Adams, housewife and receptionist / secretary. Raised in Newport News, Virginia

My CPA told me I was not eligible to have an IRA. It was a big mistake!

Name withheld

I wish I had started in my early 20s to save. All that money would have compounded.

Name withheld

Buying limited partnerships.

Don Gruitt, computer programmer, retired. Raised in West Virginia

Chris Gruitt, computer programmer, retired. Raised in Virginia

When I was young, I ran up a lot of credit card debt.

Name withheld, teacher

The biggest mistake I made with my finances was not preparing sooner in life for anything. When I was younger, I always felt like I never had enough money to invest or save, so why bother. At the time, I was a single mom with four kids and never felt I had enough money and, looking back, I could have done more saving.

Fran Laux, computer systems analyst, retired. Raised in Los Angeles, California

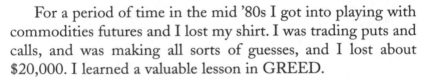

For a period of time in the mid '80s I got into playing with commodities futures and I lost my shirt. I was trading puts and calls, and was making all sorts of guesses, and I lost about $20,000. I learned a valuable lesson in GREED.

Bill Erbach, Sr., clergyman. Raised in Kearny, New Jersey

Martha Erbach, professor of nursing. Raised in Suffolk, Virginia

Buying a new automobile. It's the worst investment in the world.

Bill Graves, association financial manager, retired. Raised in Rhode Island

Jo Graves, receptionist, retired. Raised in Massachusetts

I think if I had gotten into investments 10 or 15 years sooner, I would have been better off.

Name withheld, 67. chemist

Spouse, 65. librarian

I bought a condominium about 10 years ago, and it was hard to unload. I was single and I could have rented an apartment and spent less money overall.

Faye Wood, software engineer. Raised in Elon College, North Carolina

Thomas Wood, procurement executive. Raised in Battle Creek, Michigan

We didn't invest in the right kind of investments early on. We were afraid to take more risk early in our marriage. We've always saved systematically, but we were buying savings bonds and bank CDs—very secure things. Only later did we invest in stocks. Looking back, if we had taken more risk we would have done a lot better.

Name withheld, federal civil servant, retired

Spouse, retired military

I put money away in my daughter's name for college and now I'm being penalized because she can't get financial aid.

Bill Perrick, salesperson. Raised in Scranton, Pennsylvania

Sandi Perrick, teacher. Raised in Washington, DC

I tried to play the stock market by myself—and lost my fannie!

Robert Daugherty, retired from military, retired real estate. Raised in Washington, DC

Muriel Daugherty, housewife. Raised in Virginia

I should have started a standard, monthly investing program sooner. I began one when I was in my 20s but I stopped when I got married. It wasn't until I was in my late 30s that I restarted with a dedicated effort.

Jerry White-Partain, systems analyst. Raised in Chatanooga, Tennessee

Camille White-Partain, V.P. of consulting firm. Raised in New York, New York

When I was in college and got my first credit card, I got in debt and it took me a while to get out of it. I learned credit card debt was a burden.

Diana D., software developer. Raised in Fairfax, Virginia

When I was in college and got my first credit card, I got in debt and it took me a while to get out of it. I learned credit card debt was a burden.

Having credit cards, because it's too easy to get carried away and then you have debt to pay . . . it is a vicious cycle once you begin using them.

Zandra Kern, personnel management specialist. Raised in Warren, Michigan

We ran up too much debt on our credit cards. My mother had one credit card, and she only had it for ID purposes, because she couldn't write a check anywhere without it.

Loni McConchie, administrative assistant. Raised in Easton, Maryland

Michael McConchie. Raised in Washington, DC

When my mother was alive, she put her house in the name of my sister and me. She passed away before we could change it back, and now we are going to have to pay large capital gains taxes.

Karen Bretthauer, systems accountant for Department of Agriculture. Raised in Albany, New York

---

We got involved in real estate investments when the tax law provided great tax shelters for real estate investments. We got so enamored and emotionally involved with real estate that we bought more and more . . . and then when the tax law changed, we were in very deep and as it turned out, several of the properties were not easily marketed when we wanted to unload.

Name withheld, IBM retiree. Raised in Rochester, New Jersey

Not taking even a little bit of risk in my finances when I was younger. I didn't start taking risks till my late 40s.

Robert Warren, consulting actuary. Raised in Buffalo, New York

Christine Warren, homemaker. Raised in Buffalo, New York

I loaned my daughter $10,000—it was money I couldn't afford to loan out. I took it from my retirement plan. I never got it back and so I had to pay taxes on it and I lost my retirement money.

Name withheld, secretary

We bought into a travel club recommended to us by some friends. We spent $2,000, and a couple of years later, when we were going to use the travel club's benefits, the company went belly up.

Name withheld, retired from military

------------------------ §§ ------------------------

My husband once bought a stock on a hot tip, and he lost $5,000. The investment went from bad to worse and we lost every penny. He learned real fast.

Paula Zimberg, former federal employee, now a real estate agent. Raised in Tarheel, North Carolina

------------------------ §§ ------------------------

Twenty years ago I was working for a non-profit organization that offered a retirement plan called a 403(b) and I didn't participate to the maximum. And I should have been more careful about which investment I chose in the plan. It took me a long time to accept risk when it comes to investing.

Name withheld, website designer

------------------------ §§ ------------------------

Trading in options. It made me too nervous and it was overwhelming trying to deal with options on a daily basis.

Name withheld, manager

I made two mistakes: Prior to coming to Washington, DC, I was a university professor. When I moved to Washington, I took money out of my retirement plan to buy a house and I had to pay big penalties on the taxes. I have no intention of doing that again. And when I was starting out, I put money into government bonds instead of mutual funds. I should have invested more, and not kept such large amounts in my savings account.

Name withheld, program manager

Spouse, administrative assistant

My biggest mistake was not saving and investing earlier in life.

L.A. Quezada, management analyst. Raised in Pittsburg, California

My biggest mistake was not saving and investing earlier in life.

Wish I started saving and investing earlier!

Gene Lorah, retired. Raised in Reading, Pennsylvania

Before I became a more savvy investor, I invested a sum of money and withdrew from the account as it grew, even though I didn't need the extra money. I never let the interest compound!

Name withheld

I should have gone to see an advisor earlier, too. I should have gone 20 years ago.

Friedel Groene, vice president in charge of electronic hardware manufacturing. Raised in Germany

---

I started way too late. As a young naval officer, I once got a $100 raise. Someone tried to convince me to invest half of it in stocks. I didn't—it was the worst mistake I made!

Larry Gallion, U.S. Navy (retired). Raised in Nebraska

We got a late start. We were both teachers, struggling with children. Wish we had started investing much earlier. Once we started we hardly missed the money!

Larry Sasscer, college professor. Raised in Arlington, Virginia

---

Having credit card debt—without a doubt. Everything I bought, I paid an additional 15%, 16%, or 17% interest, so I paid that much extra for everything I purchased. Since I was paying those bills off, I wasn't saving any money either. I started saving later than I should have.

Name withheld. Raised in Birmingham, Michigan

I started late!

Ed Napier, program manager. Raised in Virginia

I invested in some limited partnerships, but when the tax laws changed they became bad investments and I couldn't write off the losses.

Name withheld, IRS employee

Spouse, homemaker

I once bought two rental properties, but I did not consider the tax consequences of depreciation. As a consequence, when I sold the properties I had a big tax bill.

Hank Baker, engineer. Raised in Lucinda, Pennsylvania

Betty Baker, retired nurse. Raised in Broackway, Pennsylvania

I wish I had started earlier to save.

Dick Burke, retired. Raised in many places, as Dad was in the Army.

The Smartest Thing I Ever Did

The Smartest Thing I Ever Did

I didn't change jobs. I committed to a military service career at 27, my seventh year in the Air Force. By staying for 29 years, I became entitled to a retirement income equal to almost 75% of my base pay. Had I left the service and took jobs with different employers, as many workers do these days, I would never have received such an excellent retirement benefit.

Michael F. Burke, retired from Air Force, now working as a defense analyst with a large technical corporation. Born in Saratoga Springs, New York

Elinor K. Burke, former Air Force nurse, now a printmaker. Born in Springfield, Massachusetts

---

I found myself in a job with a good 401(k) and I invested to the max. And I also got into an overall investment plan on a regular basis.

Jackie Peluso, federal government employee. Divorced. Raised in Rockville, Maryland

---

We opened IRAs first, when they were tax beneficial to us, putting in the maximum amount. When they were no longer tax-deductible, we started saving through the payroll deduction plan at my wife's work. It grew to a sizeable amount in ten years.

Charles Canard, widowed. Raised in Warrenton, Virginia

The smartest thing I ever did? Marry my wife.

Frank DeCola, 58. auto sales. Raised in Washington, DC

Kathryn DeCola, 45. teacher. Raised in Alabama

Two things. Buying a home and taking out a large mortgage. And when I got married, we started saving the maximum amount allowed in a retirement program, both at the company and in supplemental programs.

David Webb, executive with a gas industry research organization. Raised in Lubbock, Texas

Jean Webb, homemaker. Raised in Arab, Alabama

After buying a house, I started a restaurant and catering business, and have done quite well.

Heinrich Hofmann, caterer. Raised in Persenbeurg, Austria

Anna R. Hofmann, caterer. Raised in Minas Gerais, Brazil

I socked major amounts of money into a 401(k) and 403(b) at my jobs years ago. The money has appreciated greatly.

Bea Blacklow, epidemiologist. Raised in Elmont, Long Island

Roger Blacklow, political coordinator. Raised in Washington, DC

I made my own personal financial well being a first priority.

Barbara Ramee, travel accounting administrator. Raised in Meriden, Connecticut

Probably going to a financial advisor. I was trying to make IRA investments and buy mutual funds but I didn't know what I was doing. I went to an advisor; they changed everything. I probably couldn't have retired if it wasn't for their help.

Jerry Jones, formerly an operating engineer. Raised in Tulsa, Oklahoma

Karen Johnson, flight attendant. Raised in Newport, Rhode Island

Married my second wife, who is a better influence on my money.

William Hillman, formerly with the U.S. Department of Education. Raised in Paulsboro, New Jersey

Helen Hillman, municipal worker, retired. Raised in New River, Virginia

I changed to another company when I realized I needed to do something for retirement.

Willis H. Martin, systems engineer. Raised in New Freedom, Pennsylvania

Marcia G. Martin, travel agent. Raised in York, Pennsylvania

We were not conservative about investing. I grew up knowing about the stock market because my grandfather had bought DuPont stock, and he gifted it to us, which enabled me to get an education.

Pat Black, computer programmer. Raised in Baltimore, Maryland

Contacting a financial planner. We inherited some funds, and we set it up in a portfolio to get us on the right track.

Howard Gaidsick, middle management with the U.S. Government. Raised in Seattle, Washington

Barbara Gaidsick, registered nurse. Raised in Baltimore, Maryland

When we first started out we put aside a certain percentage for savings, and we've never touched it or worried about it. It has really grown.

Name withheld, business consultant. Raised in Tempe, AR

Spouse, physician. Raised in Tulsa, Oklahoma

I put money into my investments each month before I pay the bills. It's smarter than investing what's left over.

Charles Hottel, computer specialist. Raised in Suitland, Maryland

I set goals and also got help from a professional advisor.

Name withheld, project manager. Raised in Allen Park, Michigan

Spouse, teacher

Probably getting a financial advisor. It gives you an insight into investment possibilities and takes the mystery out of it.

Neil Walp, retired regional economic planner. Raised in Bloomsburg, Pennsylvania

Mary Walp, retired credit analyst. Raised in Lightstreet, Pennsylvania

---

The smartest thing I've ever done is to get into the market and start to buy mutual funds. And also going to a financial planner.

Name withheld, software engineer. Raised in Woodbridge, Virginia

---

When the opportunity for the 401(k) was available, I invested the maximum amount.

Name withheld, software project manager for FDIC. Raised in Batesville, Missouri

---

I just save as much as I can.

Mark Danisewicz, Chief Financial Officer of major corporation. Kinnelon, New Jersey

Karen A. Danisewicz, homemaker. Raised in Springfield, Virginia

---

Smartest thing I ever did? Married my wife.

Name withheld, broadcaster, Voice of America

Spouse, retired nurse

Getting out of credit card debt. Also, it really came down to financial discipline. I tracked every single penny I spent every day and I tracked my bills, so I could quickly see how much I was paying in interest to credit card companies. I spent less day to day, so it helped me pay down my credit card bills. I was motivated because, by paying down credit card bills, in essence I gave myself a $200 raise!

Name withheld. Raised in Birmingham, Michigan

---

§§

Getting a financial planner was the smartest thing.

Bill Harper, retail manager. Raised in McKeesport, Pennsylvania

Shirley Harper, executive secretary. Raised in Front Royal, Virginia

---

§§

I was diagnosed with lung cancer and had a lung removed last year. A couple years before I was diagnosed, we got life insurance for me. Prior to that, I had no coverage. As traumatic as the situation was, it would have been so much worse had we not had a financial plan. We have two teenage daughters and a house, and if the worst happened, Tom would be okay thanks to our plan. Thank goodness we made a few plans for down the road. People should start early and be prepared for the worst. And it's not enough for the man—women have to be prepared, too. I couldn't go out and buy life insurance now. You hear people talk about planning, but they don't act on it. They should—now.

Ann, pharmacist

Give your retirement money to a financial advisor. Get professional advice.

Kathryn Coleman, President/CEO of a credit union, retired. Raised in Alexandria, Virginia

Vic Coleman, telephone company plant supervisor, retired. Raised in Pittsburgh, Pennsylvania

We lived off one spouse's income and invested the other paycheck.

Name withheld, computer systems manager

Spouse, manager of operations

Went to a financial planning seminar.

Kathleen Keim, international economist. Raised in Milwaukee, Wisconsin

My son, Kevin, was born in 1970. I was 27 at the time. We started a college fund for him right away, but we didn't have much money. So I started by putting $100 into a stock mutual fund. My wife and I then collected our change each day. It added up to about $60 a month, so twice a year, we'd put that change into the fund. We did that for 18 years—adding about $700 a year to the fund. When Kevin was ready for college, that fund was worth $53,000. I was shocked, totally amazed. I had almost half the tuition paid for both Kevin and my daughter Carrie without even trying! Anytime anyone asks about savings, that's the example I bring up. And the best part is that we didn't need to use the money for college, so it's still invested!

And all this was done with no kind of disciplined savings plan—just the loose change out of my pocket that I never missed. Even today I still have a little cup on my dresser and every night I still empty my pockets into the cup. That money goes straight into my mutual funds.

Charlie Smith, owner of chain of dry cleaners. Raised in Washington, DC

Carol Smith, nurse administrator. Raised in Boston

Went to a financial advisor.

Jovita Franco, sales representative. Raised in Manila, Philippines

Don Franco, veterinarian. Raised in Trinidad, West Indies

We didn't buy too big of a house.

Joseph Rogers, manufacturing coordinator. Raised in Louisa, Virginia

Edna Rogers, secretary. Raised in Demarest, New Jersey

I followed my wife's advice and went to a financial advisor.

Richard Six, aerospace and electronics. Raised in Miami, Florida

---

My mother was old with Alzheimer's Disease. She had a tremendous amount of stock and we needed to find a way to pay for her nursing home costs, but the dividends from her stocks weren't paying enough. I converted my mother's stocks into mutual funds and then drew some money out of the funds at a monthly rate to pay for the nursing home. I also converted my stocks to mutual funds. When my mother passed away four years later, her portfolio was worth more than when we began—even though we were drawing $3,000 each month from the mutual funds. My brother was so impressed that he wanted to know what we were investing in; now, he is doing for himself what I did for my mother and myself, and he says that it was the best thing he'd ever done financially.

Andy Taylor, retired Officer, United States Marines. Currently an 8th grade social studies teacher. Raised in Camden and Margate, New Jersey

Phyllis Taylor, registered nurse, retired. Raised in Trenton, New Jersey

---

Went to a financial advisor.

Jim Irons, Army Officer, retired. Raised in Dayton, Ohio

June Irons, sales. Raised in Dayton, Ohio

At a relatively young age, I invested in my employer's retirement plan. As a result, I will retire and never have to alter my lifestyle.

Name withheld

When I was young, I paid off my credit cards and never built up a balance again.

Name withheld, teacher

Worked with a financial planner.

Name withheld, director of administrative services, retired.

Spouse, secretary, retired

Married my wife. If I hadn't done that, I wouldn't have any of the discipline I've got—personal or economic. She's given me stability and perspective.

Mike Ferrier, company president and CEO. Raised in north eastern Ohio

Carol Ferrier, volunteer. Raised in Youngstown, Ohio

Smartest thing I did: Got married and agreed with my wife about savings.

Kenneth R. Gossage, retired from AT&T. Raised in Arlington, Virginia

---

Getting professional advice on how to handle our portfolio.

Bill Graves, association financial manager, retired. Raised in Rhode Island

Jo Graves, receptionist, retired. Raised in Massachusetts

My division of the company was sold in 1974 and 21 years of loyal service went up in smoke (along with the pension plan). All I had left were the 79 shares of stock in the company that I had previously purchased. So I bought another 21 shares to round it off to an even hundred. Over the years, I allowed the dividends to reinvest into more shares, and a couple of times I bought an additional share or two. The company was Travelers, and it recently merged with Citibank to form a new company called Citigroup. Thanks to my reinvestments over the past 25 years, I now own 1,385 shares in Citigroup, today worth about $87,000.

Name withheld

Seeking advice from a financial advisor was a great idea. You can get a better perspective on what more you can do with your current financial resources.

Name withheld, chemist

Spouse, librarian

Every time my husband got a raise, we took half and put it towards living expenses and we put the other half into savings. When I went to work, we lived off my husband's salary and invested my paycheck.

B. A., V.P. of specialty leasing for shopping centers. Raised in Traverse City, Michigan

D. A., field service engineer in aviation field. Raised in Lansing, Michigan

I like to shop—it's the thrill of victory to just go out there and buy. So rather than spending, my husband sat me down and said, "Why don't you be in charge of shopping for mutual funds?" He knew that psychologically I would enjoy it. So I stopped spending money and began hunting for the best buys in mutual funds.

D.R., advertising sales executive. Raised in Crofton, Maryland

D.R., management consultant. Raised in Crofton, Maryland

Smartest thing we did was to develop and execute a plan— and get the emotion out of it.

Name withheld, IBM retiree. Raised in Rochester, New Jersey

I got over the fear of risk.

Name withheld, website designer

Like everyone else, when we started out, we were broke. Each time I got a salary increase, I invested half of the net increase irrespective of any other savings plans that I already had.

Mike Ryder, program manager. Raised in Enfield, Connecticut

The main reason I don't get into trouble is because I live below my means.

Name withheld

I invested $550 to buy 100 shares of Forest Laboratories stock in April 1993 and held onto it until 1998. When I sold it, it was worth $74,000. I decided to sell because it grew so much that I started thinking about it too much—it started to affect my sleep a bit! I knew I shouldn't put all my eggs in one basket, because if the company went belly up, I'd never forgive myself. So I sold and I've slept well since.

Ralph Vick, construction supervisor. Raised in New Canaan, Connecticut, and Ferncliff, Virginia

Sherry Vick, division administrator. Raised in Lawrenceville, Virginia

I married a woman who has a similar philosophy.

Gary H. Bullis, engineer. Raised in Graham, North Carolina

Linda Bullis, homemaker—and the household's bookkeeper. Raised in Scranton, Kansas

I grew up in the Depression. My father lost his job and I remember having to help out on my uncle's farm with the harvesting. We never lived very high and he was frugal with his money. I always got the impression that you never got anywhere in this world unless you saved some money and got it working for you. So when I joined the Navy, I saved as much as I could—I didn't blow it like the other guys did. I was making $42 a month, but over a five-year period, I saved a few thousand dollars by putting money into a stock. By 1973, that stock was worth $25,312—I still have complete records—and I sold the stock and reinvested the money into two stock mutual funds. I didn't touch the money, except that in 1978, I withdrew $5,000 from one of the funds to buy a car. Fifteen years later, in May of 1993, I added $5,000 to one of the funds, and in

1996, I added another $10,000. That was it—no other transactions. Today, those two accounts are worth $677,738.88. I'm sorry I took out the money for that Volkswagen. I would have been better off to have borrowed the money and left my investment alone. I didn't understand what compound interest was, or how it worked. I was playing around buying speculative stocks. Some gained and some lost, but nothing was making money like my mutual funds. So after a few years, I just decided to stop playing with stocks and I put my money into mutual funds. And I'm happy I did, because I now have $1.6 million. By the time my wife retires, we'd like to have about $2 million, so we can live on the interest alone for the rest of our lives.

Name withheld

---

§§

I was working at First and Citizens National Bank in 1964. I bought $100 worth of the bank's stock. The bank went through several mergers over the years, and today is part of Suntrust. That $100 investment is now worth more than $18,000.[76]

Dorothy Williams, educational technical assistant. Raised in McRoberts, Kentucky

---

§§

I started at 35 and didn't wait any longer. I think everyone should do some planning; most people don't. People should look at everything in long-term.

Name withheld, attorney. Raised in Westchester County, New York

Spouse, school librarian

---

[76] That's an average return of 16% per year for 35 years.

We started a monthly investment plan, and put money into our 401(k) plans at work.

Stephanie Thomas, information officer at U.S. Department of Agriculture. Raised in Springfield, VA

Brad Thomas, computer analyst. Raised in Vienna, Virginia

We also overcame our fear of investing. We are still cautious but we are trying to learn as much as we can.

Name withheld, federal civil servant, retired

Spouse, retired from military

The
Obstacles
I Faced

The Obstacles I Faced

I have been on my own since the late 1970s—raising my son since he was seven, and I'm proud of him for his accomplishments. As a single parent, there were many struggles, but somehow I came through, considering there were many rough times. The second time I was laid off (September 1985), I owned a condo and my son was a teenager. I was out of work for six months. During that time, I rarely went out to the movies, dinner, nor very many social activities, even though it may have cost only $3. I did some temp work while seeking full-time employment.

In March 1986, when I became employed again, I enrolled in the 401(k) plan. I was probably in my late 40s. I started out by contributing about 1%–3% each year, and I increased that percentage each year. The majority of the time, I brown-bagged my lunch.

It wasn't until 1987 that I bought my first new car—a Honda Civic. For the first time in a long time I had car payments—I hated it. Today, I am still driving that 12-year-old car. I am very economically conscious. I go to a cosmetology hairdressing school for my permanents and hair cuts—I would rather pay $20 for a perm than $80.

Like many single parents, there were times when I was working two jobs, just to keep abreast of daily living and raising my son. However, most times, when I received my paycheck from my second job, I would put it away, even forget about it, later adding it to my investment accounts. If I got a tax refund, I would not go out and blow it—it went into my investment accounts. By February 1995, after being laid off for the third time and from the same company, I took the pension—a whopping $228 per month. Each month, I'd put $100 or more into my investment accounts.

Today, my portfolio consists of two IRAs, a money market fund, four mutual funds, a bank CD, and a senior citizens savings account. My portfolio at present is worth a little better than $200,000. I've learned over the years to save, leave it alone, be diversified, to not dip into it, and not to put all your money into your checking account. Pay yourself first by buying investments.

I cannot stress enough to anyone how important it is to invest and save, and to learn as much as you can about financial management.

Marcia J. Crosby, librarian. Raised in Providence, Rhode Island

---

I didn't "make sacrifices" in order to save, but I did have to make some choices. Held onto cars longer, took more modest vacations. Sometimes, it was tempting to cash in my long-term investments to cover expenses. But I resisted the temptation.

Jim McDaniel, park manager. Raised in Boston, Massachusetts

Michele McDaniel, administrative assistant. Raised in Lowell, Massachusetts

---

The money I have is money I saved over the last 20 years of my working career. All the money I saved in my early years was used to pay for college educations for my children, emergencies, and other living expenses. My first job was delivering newspapers. I was 13. I retired at age 70.

I credit the good advice I received from my 8th grade teacher for my present wealth. I was good in math and sciences, but I was also asthmatic, nearsighted, and often absent from class due to my asthma. When it came time for high school, my mother suggested I take the less stressful path because of my frequent absences. But my teacher encouraged me to take the college preparatory option that emphasized math and science. In fact she absolutely refused to accept any other option.

Three years later, Japan attacked Pearl Harbor, and I joined the New Jersey State Guard, a relic of the revolution, while still a sophomore in high school. I surprised everyone by passing the physical. In my senior year, the Navy visited the school looking for men good in math. I neglected to tell them I was asthmatic, and they took me. I eventually became an aviation electronic technician, and with this training, I was able to go to college after the war. I still thank God that I had an 8th grade teacher who cared.

I have several patents to my credit, but I never made money from them because I had to sign all rights to them to the company I was working for at the time. My point, though, is that most inventions occur when you build a device and it does something other than what you intended. When this happens, don't take that as failure. Instead, ask yourself, "Can I exploit this unexpected characteristic to do something useful?" If you can say "yes" then you probably have a new invention! This is especially true if you can predict the response characteristics to observable stimulants. Unfortunately, you can't do this with the stock market, although people try. The stock market does not appear to follow the laws of physics, or any other logical process.

When I was working, one of my areas of expertise was statistical control theory. The daily fluctuations of the stock market show the classical pattern associated with an underdamped control system; *e.g.* the process is characterized by unpredictable random fluctuations. This makes planning difficult. Still, in the last 25 years of working, I contributed the maximum allowed to my retirement plan at work, and I was able to accumulate a sum sufficient to comfortably support my wife and me for the rest of our lives.

Hugh Taylor, physicist and engineer, retired. Raised in New Jersey

Although we have always been aware of the need to save and invest for our retirement years, my wife and I became rather complacent about it because at age 25 I went to work for a company that offered a guaranteed retirement income at age 65. Nonetheless, in 1971, the company decided to supplement its retirement plan by allowing employees to place up to 5% of their salary into a savings account, or to purchase shares of the company stock. I chose to purchase the stock.

Unfortunately, my division of the company was sold in 1974 and 21 years of loyal service went up in smoke (along with the pension plan. Our children would soon be going off to college, so much of the savings we had accumulated would be directed to their education. All I had left were the 79 shares of stock in the company that I had previously purchased. So I bought another 21 shares to round it off to an even hundred. Over the years, I allowed the dividends to reinvest into more shares, and a couple of times I bought an additional share or two.

We opened a retirement plan on our own with $750, and put that money into a CD. This was the mid-70s; interest rates were beginning to climb and the stock market was virtually flat. We continued to invest that $750 per year into CDs until 1984, when we began transferring those CDs as they matured into mutual funds.

In 1985, I joined the federal government, and joined the government's new Federal Employee Retirement System, and as soon as they allowed us to place our contributions into stocks, I did so, knowing this would be the only way I could accumulate enough dollars to insure a comfortable retirement. I also increased my contributions as each new raise or cost of living increase went into effect. Within three years, I was investing the maximum allowed. At the same time, my wife began placing a percentage of her salary into the 401(k) plan where she worked.

Even though we got off to a late start, systematic investing at the highest rate of return possible has insured my wife and me a comfortable retirement. By the way, remember those shares of stock I had bought back in the 1970s? I kept those shares and reinvested the dividends each quarter into more shares. The company was Travelers, and it recently merged with Citibank to form a new company called Citigroup. Thanks to my reinvestments over the past 25 years, I now own 1,385 shares in Citigroup, today worth about $87,000.

Name withheld

Reflecting on the past earning years of our life together, the conclusions we have reached are that we have lived comfortably but never beyond our means, we avoided debt except for our mortgage, we shopped for our necessities and luxuries carefully, and we always tried to save as much money as possible.

Ken Misner, retired corporate executive. Raised in Boston, Massachusetts

Geri Misner, housewife. Raised in Brooklyn, New York

I worked for the government from 1941 to 1954, and was divorced and remarried during that time. My husband retired in 1958, had a heart attack in 1960, and died in 1974. From 1960 through 1977, I typed college papers at home, and then raised my new twin granddaughters.

When my husband died in 1974, I had less than $10,000. I received $2,000 in insurance, and I had a total income of under $11,000. I invested what little money I had into stocks and earned $920 in interest and dividends in 1975. The stocks grew in value, and the companies increased their dividends; by 1997 I was earning $8,561 in dividends. This was most of my income.

My assets have risen from less than $10,000 in 1974 to six figures in 1991, and they continued to rise steadily to more than half a million dollars today. I hope my luck will continue.

Name withheld

I was raised during the Depression; I was born in 1923. I didn't realize that there was a Depression until I was a teenager. My mom tended the household chores, plus raising chickens and having a vegetable garden. I didn't realize that people tend to go to the store to buy eggs, vegetables, and a chicken for Sunday dinner.

We were taught responsibility at an early age. We helped weed the garden, feed the chickens, and gather the eggs, and we helped keep the house clean. No wonder I don't like cleaning the bathrooms to this day.

We were taught to hem skirts for fifty cents and make sun suits for children that we sold for one dollar. We also did baby sitting for a dollar a day. When I asked my mother if we could spend this month, she said no, that money was to be saved for a rainy day. I remember going to her one day when it was raining so I could spend the money, and she said that wasn't what she meant. I still have one of the small metal banks we used to store our pennies in. The side read, "A dollar in the bank is worth two in the pocket."

My Dad always said, "If you see something you want and you have the money, buy it. If you see something you want and don't have the money, don't buy it." The only finance charges we have ever paid were on the two homes we've owned. We saved for autos, paid for home furnishings in cash, and used the layaway plan. Credit cards were unknown until our later years—and even today, credit cards are used for convenience; the bills are paid in full every month.

During the war, I bought war bonds and joined a silver club saving two dollars a month. It was through these savings plans that we were able to purchase our silver flatware before we were married and to furnish our first home in 1950. The house cost $12,050.

We were married in 1946. Housing was scarce, but we found a one-room apartment next to the coal drop. In that one room we ate and slept. We watched our pennies carefully. We put money into different envelopes, each marked for the purpose of the money—rent, food, emergencies. And savings. We continued to buy savings bonds, but we also started to buy AT&T stock. It took us two years to buy one share, and whenever we could we'd splurge and buy several shares. Our goal was to buy enough shares so that we'd receive $100 in dividends per month. We figured that if we had an annual income of $1,200, we'd be sitting pretty! Remember, this was 1946!

Well, we've exceeded our goal. Today our net worth approaches $2 million. The young people today are so fortunate. They have many options for saving and investing. In our day, only the rich owned stocks, and the only mutual funds we learned about were the ones sold door-to-door by salesmen or by our fellow workers. I often wonder how much better off we would be if we had the opportunity to save in stocks, bonds, and mutual funds like young people today can do.

Name withheld

My wife and I were working on maintaining investment property while our friends were at a country club enjoying the pool. We were renovating and doing a lot of other things, too, like raising three children. We took no real vacations, except to see family. We had to focus on resisting the temptation to spend everything rather than save it. I didn't consider it a sacrifice; I considered it a choice. A lot of the times we worked as a choice while other people were doing leisure things. And that's why I didn't feel like it was hard—because it was something that I wanted to do.

Gary H. Bullis, engineer. Raised in Graham, North Carolina

Linda Bullis, homemaker—and the household's bookkeeper. Raised in Scranton, Kansas

---

I say to my sons, "Take a little bit out of your paycheck each month and forget about it and let it grow. Stick with it." I didn't and wish I had; early in my marriage I was putting away $5 per month, but stopped after four years because we had kids, bought a car, a house, etc. I wish I had continued because that was 40 years ago and imagine what I would have today had I kept saving.

Bill Erbach, Sr., clergyman. Raised in Kearny, New Jersey

Martha Erbach, professor of nursing. Raised in Suffolk, Virginia

---

We raised chinchillas on a six-acre farm. At one point, we had 700 of them. We bought the farm in 1951 for $19,000 and sold it in 1967 for $105,000, on a contract where we'd get the money bit by bit over the next eight years. In 1969, we decided that we wanted to have $45,000 of it in savings by the time the income from the contract ended—and we met our goal. We just saved as much of the money as we could, even though we were living on this money, plus using some of it to pay for our daughter's college. And we didn't have to scrimp. We had a nice car, and we had fun. People today don't know how to have fun—they don't know how to have fun without spending money. We did lots of inexpensive things and we got enjoyment out of everything we did. And I'm still having fun today! I have no regrets of any kind.

Harriet Hollway, homemaker. Raised on a farm in South Dakota "that I couldn't get off fast enough."

I was married at 28 and we divorced after 12 years. The kids were nine and ten at the time of the divorce. I didn't get much money from the settlement, because we didn't have much. We sold the house, and I got a little money from that, and my ex paid $300–$500 a month for child support. I was working for the government, so I didn't make tons of money. So we lived fairly frugally. But I was able to buy a modest home in the same area as we used to live, so my kids could attend the same schools and keep the same babysitter. I had a monthly income, no debts, and was able to raise my daughter and son. They had a family environment. My youngest went through college—and when she graduated, she got out with no debt. And I had no debt, either.

Even though I wasn't bringing in much money, I was able to save every month, if only $50 or $100. I had to stop saving when her tuition bills started, though. I always saved, even as little as $5. When she graduated, I continued to live the same lifestyle so I had a whole lot more money to save, and I was really able to put it away—to the point now where I'm able to retire within a year. Because I put money away, I will be able to get that nice place in Florida I've always dreamed of. I've worked hard and I can now reap the benefits of all my efforts all these years. I'm very much looking forward to this. I became a self-made person. I've only got a high school education, but I'm doing great because of the financial choices I made.

Mitzy Williams, supervisory program analyst for the federal government. West Virginia

My Advice For You

My Advice For You

Invest early and put as much as you can into mutual funds.
Name withheld

———————————— §§ ————————————

Get a financial planner because you don't know what you don't know.
Dick Ives, retired Naval Officer. Raised in Wellsville, New York

———————————— §§ ————————————

Make saving a regular part of living.
Dick Amann, company president. Raised in Alexandria, Virginia

———————————— §§ ————————————

Start saving early. Pay yourself first.
Phyllis Parker

———————————— §§ ————————————

Get started saving as early as you can. Live sensibly within your means.
Max Thomas, retired Army Officer and consultant. Raised in Indiana

Start a regular savings plan and think before you buy.

Kathryn Coleman

Pay off your credit cards every month. Be conservative with spending.

Name withheld

Save on a regular basis, even if it's $10 a week, and invest it into a good mutual fund. But just save something. Get good financial advice from a planner; ignore your friends' advice.

Jody Pearce, housewife. Raised in Pennsylvania

Don Pearce, construction. Raised in Pennsylvania

Save regularly. Set a major goal that you want to achieve. Get into the habit of saving. Save anywhere. Just make sure you're saving something.

Name withheld

Start early. Do whatever you can to save as much money as you can. Pay yourself first.

Name withheld

Start saving early and be willing to make some sacrifices.
Wilbur Jenkins, firefighter. Raised in Silver Spring, Maryland

---

Do not live beyond your means.
Marian Kilgore

Start saving as early as you can and as much as you can.
Kathleen Keim

Learn more about money and how it works. Understand how to use money to your advantage.
Jim McDaniel

Start early. Do whatever you can to save as much money as you can. Pay yourself first.
Name withheld, business automation consultant
Spouse, law enforcement

Start talking to a financial advisor early in life.
Jim Irons

Save as much as you can.

Name withheld

Start saving early.

Harry R. Tansill, federal employee, retired. Raised in Washington, DC

Start saving as soon as you can in life. And get used to doing it.

Darlene Joyce

Stick with investing and put the maximum you are allowed to contribute in your 401(k) plan.

Raymond L. Cogswell

Plan for the long term.

Name withheld

Don't trade stocks every day.

Lillian Brown

Always consider the long-range effect of moving money. Don't get out of stocks just because the market doesn't look good today. And start saving early in life. Setting up some systematic method of savings is the best way.

Name withheld

Do not move your money around, just leave your investments alone. Save more, save earlier, and save as much as you can.

Jovita S. Franco, sales representative. Raised in Manila, Philippines

Get yourself a financial advisor or make sure you know what you're doing. Start early and let your money grow.

Joseph Rogers, manufacturing coordinator. Raised in Louisa, Virginia

Edna Rogers, secretary. Raised in Demarest, New Jersey

Learn as much as you can about money. After you choose your investments, stick with them. Consider using a financial advisor. Start saving early in life.

Barbara Ramee, travel accounting administrator. Raised in Meriden, Connecticut

Start as early as you can.

Vivian Rosskamm, teacher trainer. Raised in suburban Maryland

---

Do your homework. And identify your objectives.

Ginny Geiling, part owner of contractor company. Raised in Mamaroneck, New York

---

Be very cautious about moving your money around.

Richard W. Voelker

If you're like me, I recommend you talk to a financial advisor . . . now.

Richard Six, aerospace and electronics. Raised in Miami, Florida

---

Save all you can in stocks.

Name withheld

Put away at least 10% of your gross income and don't touch it.

John Barrow, public safety employee. Raised in Columbia, Maryland

Understand the powerful relationship between time and compounding and get general knowledge of what it takes to achieve financial success. Your best bet is to hire someone to help you make these decisions, unless you are really savvy and disciplined to do the work yourself.

John DeBerardinis, adult education administration (retired). Raised in Thompson, Connecticut

Take full advantage of your 401(k) and look for long-term return. It's not going to happen for you in a savings account.

Name withheld

Put the maximum into your retirement plan, and do not attempt to take it out.

Elizabeth Barnhill

Get in a 401(k) plan as soon as possible and save to the max.

John Lambert, sales manager. Raised in Virginia

Save from day one, no matter what the amount. Just do it and make it your first priority.

Ann Dudley, pharmacist. Raised in Shelby, North Carolina

Get as much of a mortgage as you can for as long as you can. Using someone else's money is always better than using your own.

Michael F. Burke, retired from Air Force, now working as a defense analyst with a large technical corporation. Raised in Saratoga Springs, New York

———————————— §§ ————————————

Always be house poor. Get as big a mortgage as you can afford because, over time, the tax deduction is a tremendous financial advantage.

David Webb

———————————— §§ ————————————

Get a house you can afford and as long a mortgage as possible.

Marty C.

———————————— §§ ————————————

Carry a mortgage because mortgage money is the least expensive money you can get.

Willis H. Martin

———————————— §§ ————————————

Don't become house poor.

Shirley Hurst

Understand that the mortgage is only the first part of owning a home. Be prepared for the maintenance and monthly upkeep, and have money for contingencies and major repairs, such as the plumbing, heating, roof, etc.

William Harper, retail manager. Raised in McKeesport, Pennsylvania

---

Don't buy more of a house than you can afford.

Kathryn M.

Always pay your credit cards off every month; never leave a balance. And save for retirement with IRAs, but be sure to keep cash on hand for emergencies.

Name withheld

Be aware of your income vs. your expenses. Don't spend what you don't have.

Name withheld

Pay your bills. Don't ever put yourself in a position where you owe interest to a credit card. Make sure you have a little more money coming in than going out.

Elizabeth Roderick, admin / personnel. Raised in New Jersey

Don't procrastinate.

Don Gruitt, computer programmer, retired. Raised in West Virginia

Don't forget about the bills that aren't monthly, like your insurance premiums and annual gift-giving. Look at your bills for a year and set aside the money to pay for them.

Name withheld

Invest instead of save.

Mike Ferrier

Work as many jobs as you need to pay your bills. Get an education.

Dan Novak

Get organized, be disciplined, stay in control. If you are married, make sure you both know what is going on, have common goals, and trust one another.

Name withheld

Show your children how to do it.

Name withheld

Pay off your credit cards every month if you can. Otherwise, at least make a serious dent in the balance. Don't spend more then you earn. Keep track of your expenditures so you can make room for savings.

Peter Callejas, engineer, retired. Raised in Newburyport, Massachusetts

---

Learn the principal of compounding and take advantage of it.

Frank DeCola

If you have the opportunity to get into a company retirement plan where you work, do it.

Virgina Endicott, teacher. Raised in Globe, Arizona

Don't rack up bills you can't pay at the end of the month.

Martin Bell

The sooner you plan and the more money you put away, the better off you'll be. You'll even be able to retire earlier.

Fred D., project executive. Raised in San Mateo, California

Invest the maximum amount you can.

Name withheld

Start early, even if it's a small amount. Time is the biggest asset you have.

Name withheld

Meet with a planner early in the game. Someone who gives proper advice and looks at your portfolio at least once a year.

Friedel Groene, vice president in charge of electronic hardware manufacturing. Raised in Germany

---

Save to the maximum extent possible.

Name withheld

Seek professional advice on how to select investments.

name withheld

Pay yourself first.

Mark Danisewicz

If you have 401(k) at work, max it out. Build yourself a four-legged chair: pension, social security, a retirement plan, and additional investing.

Name withheld

Don't spend every dime from every paycheck all at once. Do something to save.

Linda Jackie

Contribute the most you can to savings.

Kathleen Hoyt

Stop buying things you don't really need and put the money aside and invest it. You need to separate *needs* from *wants*.

Name withheld

Don't worry about how much you're investing, just be more concerned about saving money.

Karl W. Ruyle, manager, Central Intelligence Agency. Raised in Ottawa, Illinois and Canitou Springs, Colorado

Start saving as soon as you can and have a structured plan for doing it.

Carol Wyant, program analyst. Raised in Beltsville, Maryland

Save something all of the time. No matter how little you think you're making.

Bill Graves

Make sure you give your investments a chance to make money for you after you buy them. Work hard and be frugal. Enjoy, but be frugal.

George Gentili

Start saving yesterday. Whatever you save, don't ever, ever touch it. And I think you should keep close tabs on what your parents are doing because they can be taken in a heartbeat. Direct your parents to good financial advice if you can't give it to them yourself.

Joseph Ivers

Stocks and bonds aren't as risky as I believed—find out about them! Get your kids involved in learning about stocks and bonds, too. And find out what your parents are doing, how they are living and getting along.

Robert Warren

Involve your kids in the economics of the family and make them aware of how hard it is to earn a buck.

Start planning for how your parents are going to be handled if something happens. Go to someone who understands the markets and be willing to follow that advice.

Herb Mendelsohn

When you give kids an allowance make sure they save some of it. Teach them to save.

Joe Schuck, retired federal employee. Raised in St. Paul, Minnesota

---

Talk to your parents about their finances and their long-term care needs. And for yourself, start saving early and don't loan money to family members in detriment of yourself.

Name withheld

Get into the habit of saving on a regular basis, no matter how much it is. And talk with your parents to find out what they want done, from funeral arrangements to estate planning.

Name withheld

Don't spend what you don't have. And talk to your parents and children so they know what's going on.

Name withheld

Call a financial advisor.

Paula Zimberg

Invest early and often.

Name withheld

Find a way to save as much as you can and as early as you can. Get it into stocks and use the magic of compounding.

Name withheld

Something is better than nothing and the earlier you start the better.

Helene

Get in early, contribute as much as you can, don't try to time the market, be a long-term investor, and don't think short-time when you get to retirement. You're going to live 20 years or so after you retire, so don't think short-term.

Jay

Start early.

Name withheld

––––––––––– §§ –––––––––––

Be willing to take risk, and be sure to have the money taken off the top of your paycheck—if you don't see it, you don't miss it, and won't want to spend it.

Name withheld

––––––––––– §§ –––––––––––

Talk to a financial advisor, and learn what you can about retirement planning so you can make the best informed decisions possible. Don't be trapped into thinking of money in the old way. For example: people still pay off mortgages. You should invest that money into mutual funds instead.

Name withheld

––––––––––– §§ –––––––––––

Make sure that you are diversified in your investments.

Charlie Shipp

––––––––––– §§ –––––––––––

My advice would be to start saving as soon as you start working. Don't wait—that's the key to it all.

L.A. Quezada, management analyst. Raised in Pittsburg, California

Start as young as you can.

Name withheld

Start a monthly investment program with whatever money you can, as early in your life as you can.

Karen S. Griffin, executive assistant. Raised in Newton, Massachusetts

---

Put your money in a 401(k) program through work. Set aside money for yourself first. Begin saving now. Put off purchasing wild extravagances and use the money for financial security. Plan to live to be 100 years old.

Tim M.

AFTERTHOUGHTS

In Our Own Words

In order to present you with the thoughts and feelings of "ordinary people," several members of my staff joined me in conducting interviews with hundreds of my firm's clients. As we reviewed, organized, and assembled our interview notes, patterns clearly emerged, and you've seen the results within these pages.

As we were concluding the project, I began to wonder what impact—if any—the interviews had on my staff. After all, they each spent hundreds of hours interviewing and talking with dozens and dozens of my firm's clients. Some of the interviews lasted more than an hour. What was their reaction, I wondered. Did talking with these folks have any impact on them?

I put that question to each of my staff, and their responses follow:

Renee West, 44. Married, with one daughter.

I got extremely anxious after listening to our clients. They saved despite all odds, did without, didn't go into debt, and they did it all on teacher's salaries, government salaries, and so on. So, I made an appointment with you after I yelled at Kirt [her husband] for not saving enough. Really, it did effect me in that they did it on much less money than I earn. I really started thinking about where I'll be later in life. Many had spouses in poor health (I've been through that) and they are caring for them, not seeming to complain. Most didn't think they had "a lot," none complained about anything, yet they came from the Depression era and seem happy for what they do have. They all thought their children had and wanted things much too fast "these days." "Wish I started saving earlier" . . . their response and mine.

Lisa Korhnak, 30. Married, expecting her first child.

I enjoyed conducting these interviews a lot. The folks I talked with were very friendly and had interesting stories to share (sometimes they didn't think their stories were interesting, but they really were). I talked with ordinary people of middle- to upper-class backgrounds who made small sacrifices (some more than others) to save and invest their money to create wealth. Much of what they said goes along with what I believe, which is the Edelman philosophy of saving, paying off debts, starting early, and investing wisely with a financial advisor. The one thing I kept hearing from everyone I talked with is to start saving early, even if it's just a little bit. It made me think about where my money is being spent and where I can cut back so I can save more for the future.

Rosa Zediker, 26. Single.

I really enjoyed conducting the interviews. The people I spoke with shared really interesting stories, and they really made me stop and think about my retirement and how I will handle my situation when the time comes.

Michael Volpe, 47. Married, with two children.

My father-in-law passed away almost three years ago around the age of 77; he died without hardly leaving any money or material possessions, although he successfully raised five kids; I was struck by the fact that your older clients who were almost his contemporaries were in much better shape than him financially; they scrimped and saved and invested wisely, and were either looking forward to or currently enjoying their "golden years." Quite a contrast.

My wife and I have had the foresight to put away quite a bit of money for our retirements since we got married in 1978 in our early 20s. And as I look at the amounts we've accumulated so far, and after having spoken to some of your clients who are slightly older and started saving and investing a little later in life than we did, I realize now how fortunate we were to have had the discipline to put some of our money away and not blow it on fancy cars, expensive jewelry, or unnecessary trips.

The few clients I did interview who were in debt, divorced, or were starting very late in life to put money away for their retirements, seemed to have such a sadness in their voices, like they knew they made the mistake of a lifetime, one which they would never be able to recapture again.

Bruce E. Mattare, 32. Single.

I thought it was an excellent experience to hear firsthand from people about how important it is to start saving early and to save as much as you can. All the people who started early were thankful that they did, and they were amazed at how much money they accumulated over the years. And most of them were average wage earners.

By talking with so many successful people, all of whom are my elders, the importance of saving for my future was strongly reinforced. Also, talking to people who became successful by saving money over long periods made the process seem more real. I came to understand that saving for one's retirement is not a short journey. It has always been hard for me to fathom the idea that I might one day have a sizable retirement portfolio. This project made it easier for me to see that it takes many years, and that in the beginning, the nest egg is small. Before this, you could have told me until you were blue in the face that compounding over time will produce large sums of money, but until I saw it in action, it didn't really hit home.

It's too bad more young people don't have conversations with people like these. I think it would help them to realize that becoming wealthy is far less difficult than they imagine. Talking with the survey respondents and hearing their stories, solidified my goal and reinforced my determination to stick with it.

Kathy Renzetti, 29. Married, with one child.

It made me realize the importance of starting early. I feel pretty fortunate at this age to have so much knowledge about money and investing. It also made me realize that a little sacrifice now pays off later. The people I spoke with had saved and sacrificed when they were younger so they could enjoy retirement. They all seemed happy with the decisions they had made.

My Own (Final) Words

Surveying thousands of our clients, then interviewing hundreds more, was an elaborate, yet very rewarding, process. As these pages reflect, we learned a lot about achieving financial success and, as you can see from my staff's comments on pages 301–304, we learned a lot about ourselves, too.

This book has shown you the common traits and habits of our firm's clients, to help you see how you can secure a financially successful future. But as I finished the manuscript and set about the book's final layout, something was bothering me, and it's taken me quite some time to realize what it is. And, in the end, it's two things.

First, I anticipated that the chapter, "The Obstacles I Faced" would be far-and-away the most gripping. After all, I know my clients well, and many of them have lived through harrowing times. Many grew up during the Depression, and came of age during World War II. They lived through the Korean War, the Cold War, and Vietnam. Many of my clients have severe health problems. Others lost a wife or husband while still young. Several lost school-age children to accidents or illness; one client's child vanished and was never seen again. Some have disabled children who require massive medical, financial, and emotional support. Some have told me of abuse they'd suffered as children, or physical attacks they've endured. One was tortured during his seven-year captivity as a Vietnam POW. Another's son was one of the few American soldiers killed in the Gulf War. A third had a son arrested for murder. One client broke his neck in an auto accident and is paralyzed from the chest down. Another lost her sight in her 30s. Two lost everything when Hurricane Agnes hit, and many more were forced to start over after tornadoes destroyed their homes.

As I said, these are gripping stories, and I anticipated that their descriptions—in their own words—would make great reading. But none of the hundreds of clients we talked to related any of these stories. It's not that these stories don't exist, or that my clients were being coy or trying to keep these matters private. Instead, they explained to me that they simply don't consider their life's experiences to have been, well, obstacles. In one memorable exchange, I asked one client why he failed to mention in our interview that he was forced to drop out of medical school when his father's business failed. He reflected for a moment, and replied, "Oh, that. Well, I don't see that as an obstacle, I guess. Everyone goes through this sort of thing, one way or another."

And that's how everyone felt. They didn't experience *obstacles;* they experienced *life.* Everyone has challenges and everyone faces obstacles, my clients believe. The difference is that they don't dwell on them. They don't offer them up as excuses. They don't wave them in front of everyone, demanding special preference or attention. And they certainly don't let life defeat them. The more I came to realize how uniform they were in their outlook, the more humbled I became. And that's when it hit me: this is, indeed, gripping.

My second epiphany came after I realized the first. With my new perspective, I re-read their comments. And it was then that I noticed another trait that they all shared. Peppered throughout the transcripts were two words: *luck* and *lucky.*

Time and again, my clients said they were lucky. They said their success was due to luck, to having been born in the right time, in the right town, to the right parents. Or going to the right school, getting the right job, marrying the right girl (or guy). Sometimes they rejoiced over their luck in choosing the right stock, or making the right investment. Virtually none of my clients were willing to admit that their hard work, their years of sacrifice, their decades of dedication were responsible for the success they now enjoy.

I know better. I know that luck has nothing to do with their success, and I know that my clients are not at all lucky. And I also know one other thing: I am the luckiest guy in the world for having the privilege of knowing them.

About the Author

Ric Edelman, CFS, RFC, CMFC, CRC is one of the nation's best-known and most successful financial advisors. He is on the faculty of Georgetown University, a state- and AICPA-approved instructor for continuing professional education and a member of the NASD Board of Arbitrators. He was named Financial Planner of the Year three times by World Invest Corporation, and in 1994 *Washingtonian* magazine named him one of the top financial experts in the Washington, D.C., area.

Ric has been the subject of feature stories in *The Washington Post, Dow Jones Investment Advisor, Registered Representative, The Washington Times, Washington Business Journal* and *Wall Street Computer Review,* and he has been quoted by *The Wall Street Journal, The Washington Post, Fortune magazine, Financial Planning on Wall Street, Bottom Line Personal* and *Family Circle.*

In addition to Mr. Edelman's substantial financial expertise, he is a highly-regarded financial educator and communicator. Ric is one of the most sought-after speakers for seminars, conventions and conferences across the country, and he is widely acknowledged as one of the most entertaining and informative speakers in the personal finance field.

Ric is the popular host of radio's *The Ric Edelman Show* (for which he won the Washington, D.C., A.I.R. Award for Best Talk Show Host), which airs on WMAL Radio AM630 in Washington (Saturdays 10am-noon EST). He also hosts two call-in television shows, one on the national America's Voice cable network (Mondays 9pm EST) and another on the DC—area's Newschannel 8 (Mondays 7pm EST), writes a syndicated news column, and publishes a monthly newsletter. Ric created one of the most popular personal financial web sites at www.ricedelman.com. Ric also has produced a popular series of video tapes and audio cassettes on a variety of personal finance topics.

Whatever the medium—print, broadcast, electronic or live presentation—Ric is able to explain difficult financial concepts in plain English, and he is consistently rated as one of the best communicators in his field.

In addition to his achievements as a financial planner and educator, Ric has created one of the most impressive business organizations in the nation. Winners of 40 professional, business and community service awards—including "1994 Service Business of the Year" Award by the Fairfax Va. Chamber of Commerce—The Edelman Financial Center Inc., today invests $1.5 billion in client assets and was three times named by *Inc.* magazine as the fastest-growing privately-held financial planning firm in the country (1995-1997).

The Edelman Financial Center Inc., founded by Ric Edelman in 1987, is a professional group of financial planners, investment advisors and insurance counselors, mortgage professionals, educators, and business consultants who are devoted to providing the very best advice and service to clients. In recognition of these activities, Ric has five times been named as a finalist for the Washington, D.C., Entrepreneur of the Year Award (he still hasn't won).

12450 Fair Lakes Circle
Suite 200, Fairfax, VA 22033-3808
(703) 818-0800
FAX (703) 818-1910
REdelman@ricedelman.com

www.ricedelman.com

Also Available from the Author

Ric's National Best-Sellers "The New Rules of Money" and "The Truth About Money"

Both books were on the *New York Times*, and *Washington Post* best-seller lists! In bookstores everywhere, also available on audio cassette by HarperAudio.

Seminars on Video

How to Choose a Financial Advisor
Learn how planners are paid, what they do, how to assess credentials, the 12 key questions to ask when interviewing planners, and more.

How to Handle Your IRA, 401(k), 403(b) and Thrift Plan
Learn the right way to invest for retirement, Goldilocks Rules, when never to invest in an IRA, and more. Try to pass Ric's IRA quiz!

How to Invest in Mutual Funds
Learn about the rankings trap, how to choose funds, all about fees, beta, standard deviation, and the Top 10 mistakes fund investors make.

Protecting Against the Cost of Long-Term Care
Learn how to protect yourself from the biggest financial risk facing retirees.

Introduction to Estate Planning
This seminar teaches you how to avoid estate taxes and probate, and why simple wills can be a bad idea. Above all, you'll learn how to preserve peace in your family.

How to Achieve Financial Success
Learn why your home is not a great investment, why bond buyers are never happy, why to avoid muni bonds, and how risky investments can increase your safety.

Five Great Reasons to Carry a Big, Long Mortgage
Learn why you should obtain a big, long mortgage—and never pay it off. Plus tips that can save you tens of thousands of dollars on the biggest transaction you'll ever make!

How to Become a Successful Financial Planner
Financial planning is the best career opportunity of the decade. Now you can tap into this incredible opportunity by learning from one of the nation's top financial advisors.

Online with Ric!

Get advice from Ric and his team of professionals at: www.ricedelman.com. Sign up for Ric's free weekly newsletter!

Subscribe to Ric's Award-Winning 12-page Monthly Newsletter

Get the latest tips and information, including the best advice from Ric's award-winning radio and TV shows. This popular monthly offers practical financial advice to help you achieve personal success.

Invite Ric to Speak at Your Next Conference

Ric is one of the most entertaining speakers in the field of personal finance. Call 703-818-0800 for more information.

Ric on the Air

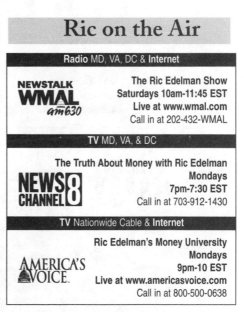

Radio MD, VA, DC & Internet

NEWSTALK **WMAL** am 630

The Ric Edelman Show
Saturdays 10am-11:45 EST
Live at www.wmal.com
Call in at 202-432-WMAL

TV MD, VA, & DC

NEWS**8** CHANNEL

The Truth About Money with Ric Edelman
Mondays
7pm-7:30 EST
Call in at 703-912-1430

TV Nationwide Cable & Internet

AMERICA'S VOICE

Ric Edelman's Money University
Mondays
9pm-10 EST
Live at www.americasvoice.com
Call in at 800-500-0638

To Order Call Toll-Free 1-888-987-PLAN

How to Give Your Child or Grandchild as Much as
$2,451,854 For Only $5,000*

You've learned that a small amount of money can grow into a small fortune, thanks to compound interest. But as simple and effective as it is, few people take as much advantage of this concept as they can. For example, few begin saving for college as soon as a child is born. And even if you were to set aside $5,000 for a newborn, it would grow over 18 years to just $27,800 (assuming 10% per year). That's hardly enough to pay for college today, let alone 18 years from now.

But imagine saving that same $5,000 for the child's retirement rather than college. With 65 years on which to compound the interest, again assuming a 10% annual return, the account would be worth not just $27,800 but more than $2.4 million!*

Although easy to understand, the tax, legal and economic obstacles prevented most of us from creating an account that could let money grow like this. But now you can do this for the benefit of your loved ones!

Introducing the Retirement InCome - for Everyone Trust®
So Innovative, it's Patented!

Your kids don't need a lot of money, and they don't need an astronomically high rate of return. All they need is a little money and an opportunity to obtain a competitive return—because time does the rest.

Through the RIC-E Trust®, you can put the power of compound interest to work for your children and grandchildren. You can establish a RIC-E Trust® for any child of any age. You don't have to be the child's parent or grandparent, and the child even can be an adult. It's perfect for newlyweds and recent graduates! You can contribute as little as $5,000 (more if you like) and the money can grow undisturbed until the child reaches retirement age (you designate the age, at least 59).

Best of all, with the RIC-E Trust®, there are no trustee fees, no investment advisory fees—and no annual income taxes for the life of the trust! Thus, all of the Trust's earnings grow tax-deferred for the benefit of the child—giving the trust the opportunity to grow to millions of dollars over the course of the child's life.

The RIC-E Trust® offers you a truly revolutionary way to help you secure the retirement future of a child you love. It's so innovative, a patent application has been filed for it.

I invite you now to learn how you can put the RIC-E Trust® to work for the important children in your life.

---

the **Retirement InCome - for Everyone** trust

Get your free copy of the Consumer Information Kit. Just call today toll-free

1-800-762-9797

I'll rush your complete kit to you, which includes the RIC-E Trust® Enrollment Form.

---

*Results based on $5,000 earning 10% per year, compounded annually. Calculation does not reflect any charges or fees that might be applicable; such charges or fees would reduce the return. This figure is for illustrative purposes only and does not reflect the actual performance of any particular investment. Investment results fluctuate and can decrease as well as increase. Figures do not take into consideration time, value of money or any fluctuation in principal. Your tax liability may vary depending on your particular circumstances. Please consult your tax advisor.

Patent No. 6,064,986

Index

☗ HarperBusiness

Books by Ric Edelman:

ORDINARY PEOPLE, EXTRAORDINARY WEALTH
The 8 Secrets of How 5,000 Ordinary Americans Became
Successful Investors—and How You Can Too
ISBN 0-06-273686-8 (paperback) • ISBN 0-694-52261-9 (audio)

Ric Edelman provides readers with the method of achieving extraordinary financial
success by using eight unconventional but proven strategies for smart investing
from his survey of 5,000 of his most successful clients.

"If you follow these simple rules, you will not only accumulate wealth for
  yourself but you will enjoy a much happier and healthier life."
—Dr. Paul B. Farrell, *CBS MarketWatch*

THE TRUTH ABOUT MONEY
Revised Edition
ISBN 0-06-095636-4 (paperback) • ISBN 0-694-51914-6 (audio)

A comprehensive, practical, "how-to" manual on financial planning, written
for anyone concerned about their financial well-being. The book discusses
investments, long-term care, planning for retirement, buying and selling your
home, how to get out of debt, how to pay for college or your daughter's wedding,
and much more. A *New York Times* bestseller.

"Conversational, clever . . . and easy to read."—*USA Today*

THE NEW RULES OF MONEY
88 Simple Strategies for Financial Success Today
ISBN 0-06-272074-0 (paperback) • ISBN 0-694-51929-4 (audio)

Tailor-made for today's economy, Edelman's 88 strategies show how to achieve
financial success, while making personal finance fun and his advice easy to put into
action.

"He's unconventional. He's contrary. But when it comes to investing, people
  listen." —*The Washington Post*

"One of the most successful financial advisors in the country."
—*Dow Jones Investment Advisor*

Available wherever books are sold, or call 1-800-331-3761 to order.